Delighting Your Customers

*Keep your customers coming
back, time and time again*

SUSAN NASH & DEREK NASH

How To Books

Also available in an expanded form as *Exceeding Customer Expectations* by Susan Nash and Derek Nash published by How To Books in 2000.

Published by How To Books Ltd,
3 Newtec Place, Magdalen Road,
Oxford OX4 1RE, United Kingdom.
Tel: (01865) 793806. Fax: (01865) 248780.
email: info@howtobooks.co.uk
http://www.howtobooks.co.uk

First edition 2001

British Library Cataloguing in Publication Data.
A catalogue record for this book is available from
the British Library.

Edited by Diana Brueton
Cover design by Shireen Nathoo Design
Cover image by PhotoDisc
Produced for How To Books by Deer Park Productions
Typeset by Kestrel Data, Exeter
Printed and bound by Cromwell Press Ltd, Trowbridge, Wiltshire

NOTE: The material contained in this book is set out in good faith for general guidance and no liability can be accepted for loss or expense incurred as a result of relying in particular circumstances on statements made in the book. Laws and regulations are complex and liable to change, and readers should check the current position with the relevant authorities before making personal arrangements.

Contents

List of Illustrations

Preface

This book is designed for anyone who is working within an organisation, whether small or large, who wants to improve standards of service to the customer. Whether you are a business owner, manager, service provider or executive, this book will provide useful tools and techniques to improve service at all levels in your organisation.

It will provide a methodology to systematically improve the service provided to customers so that customer expectations can be exceeded and your business can remain viable.

In this book we introduce a service management model with specific tools and techniques within each section.

First we define customer service in some depth, and describe a comprehensive approach to improving it. Then you will be given information, skills and techniques to raise your competency in specific areas where you may need help.

The outcome of implementing these ideas can be creating situations where you are able to delight the customer: to provide a service that far exceeds the customers' expectations. These situations become the stories that act as free PR and build a company's reputation.

The contents of this book were developed after many years of working with a broad range of organisations as they struggled to make delighting your customers a fact and not a fantasy. Good luck in this journey!

Susan and Derek Nash

1

Understanding Customer Service

As business enters the 21st century, customer service remains a fundamental factor for business success and profitability.

While most of us deal with customer service every day, either as a customer or as a service provider, many of us do not necessarily understand what constitutes good customer service. In this chapter we will lay the groundwork for the rest of the book by identifying some misconceptions about the critical components of a positive service interaction, and then by thoroughly defining customer service.

WHAT IS CUSTOMER SERVICE?

To raise awareness and to set the scene for the rest of this chapter, take a moment and answer the following questions. Choose only one answer for each question. Think about customer service in general, for instance in banks, restaurants, retail stores etc, not necessarily the context in which you provide customer service.

1 What is the biggest single reason why businesses lose customers?
   (a) new competition
   (b) indifference of one employee
   (c) word of mouth
   (d) dissatisfaction with the product

2 What percentage of dissatisfied customers *does not* complain to you about discourteous or indifferent customer service?
   (a) 48%
   (b) 65%
   (c) 78%
   (d) 96%

3 Of those customers who do complain, what percent is likely to return to that business again?

(a) 50%
(b) 70%
(c) 80%
(d) 90%

4 For the average business, what percent of annual sales comes from existing satisfied customers?
(a) 30%
(b) 10%
(c) 65%
(d) 50%

5 How much more money does it take to find a new customer instead of getting more business from an existing customer?
(a) twice as much
(b) three times as much
(c) four times as much
(d) over five times as much

6 A dissatisfied customer will tell how many people, outside of the company, about poor service received?
(a) two to three people
(b) four to six people
(c) seven to eight people
(d) over nine people, but as many as 20

CUSTOMER SERVICE QUIZ ANSWERS

The answers to this quiz were gathered from TARP (Technical Assistance Research Program) research conducted by the White House Office of Consumer Affairs and quoted in the book *How to Win Customers and Keep Them for Life* by Michael Leboeuf.

Quiz answers:
1 (b)
2 (d)
3 (d)
4 (c)
5 (d)
6 (d)

Why customers leave (question 1)

The biggest single reason why businesses lose customers is:

- Indifference of one employee – 68 per cent.

Other reasons customers choose to take their business elsewhere are:

- Dissatisfaction with the product – 14 per cent.
- New competition – 9 per cent.
- Word of mouth – 5 per cent.

This research was based on answers from customers who were asked: 'What was the factor that influenced your decision not to use this product or service again?' At the point of interaction between the customer and the service provider, the indifference of one employee was cited as the major reason customers chose to take their business elsewhere. Every individual within a company can make a significant impact, not only on the customer experience, but also on the company's service reputation in the marketplace. However, in the long term businesses obviously have to offer a comparable, competitive product that is technically adequate in order to ensure the long-term viability of the organisation.

Who complains (question 2)

Ninety-six per cent of dissatisfied customers *do not* complain to you about discourteous or indifferent customer service: we only hear from 4 per cent of our dissatisfied customers. This means that for every complaint received, there are in fact 26 other customers with problems, six of which are serious issues.

The rest either vote with their feet, and do not return, or complain to anyone else *outside* the company who will listen. In order to deliver exceptional service, we have to create the means for customers to complain to us. Only when we know about the problems will we be able to resolve them. The concept of providing our customers with the tools they can use to complain, and recovering from the complaint is covered in later chapters.

Who returns after complaining (question 3)

Of those customers who do complain, what percent is likely to return to that business again? This question has two correct answers. If the complaint is not handled effectively, only 50 per cent of customers will do business with that organisation again. When British Airways conducted their initial market research into customer perceptions, it showed that when the service delivery was acceptable, the customers were satisfied. However, when a problem occurred, only 50 per cent of the customers would return to the airline, based on the fact that their complaint was not resolved to their satisfaction. They termed this process of successfully resolving customer complaints 'recovery'. If the complaint was resolved quickly and successfully, over 95 per cent of customers would return. Effective recovery is an incredibly important service management tool. Chapter 8 discusses strategies for recovery in more detail.

Service and sales (question 4)

The most conservative data infers that over 65 per cent of annual sales comes from existing satisfied customers. Regarding service businesses and adding the factor of referrals, some businesses receive almost 100 per cent of their new business from existing satisfied customers and the referrals they make to others.

Cost of generating new business (question 5)

Research in this area has produced different results. Estimates show that it costs five to ten times as much to generate business from new customers as it does to get more business from existing customers. Despite this data, companies continue to invest large amounts of promotional money to encourage new customers to try their service or product, and then ruin the experience at the service delivery point!

Spreading the word (question 6)

The 'average' customer who has a problem tells nine to ten people about it. Approximately 13 per cent of dissatisfied customers will tell more than 20 people, personally, about the problem. Of the people they tell, each one will on average tell two to three more people. This means that usually 200–300 people personally hear about every negative service experience. A scary thought, particularly when you combine the effect of the internet where potentially 100 million people could read about the same customer service horror story!

Conversely good news does not travel as fast as bad news. On average a satisfied customer will only tell three to five people about the experience. You have to deliver much more good service to outweigh the possible negative consequences of bad service.

Conclusions

Of the six questions, how many did you answer correctly? In our research we have found that, on average, most people answer between three and four questions accurately.

From this you can see that most of us need to broaden our understanding of customer service. Let's begin to define customer service in more detail.

KNOWING WHAT MAKES US SATISFIED OR DISSATISFIED

What constitutes positive or negative customer service?

Hotels are renowned for confusing bookings. When travelling recently, the room key I was given wouldn't work because someone else was already in the room. When I went back to reception the response I was given was 'the system made a mistake'! The factors that made me dissatisfied with that experience were:

- No ownership of the problem.

- No apology.

- Blaming of the mistake onto someone/thing else.

- No resolution of the problem.

- Couldn't care less attitude.

EXERCISE

Now think of your own experiences as a customer in retail, restaurants, hotels, travel, etc. Think of a specific time when you were dissatisfied with the service you received. How did you feel? What factors contributed to your dissatisfaction? Try to separate the experience itself from the factors that caused you to feel the service did not meet your expectations.

List the factors associated with your negative experience.

On another visit to a hotel in Denver, my room reservation was once again confused, but with a twist. This time someone else was given a key to the room I was in! A poor tired business executive walked into the room and found an undressed woman cleaning her teeth. He exited the room much quicker than he entered. Thirty seconds later there was another knock at the door. The front desk manager had come up personally to apologise for the mistake and to reassure me that it would not happen again. In addition the following evening there was a personal note from the front desk manager apologising for the disturbance accompanied by a bottle of wine and a basket of cheese and crackers.

The factors that made this a satisfactory experience were:

- Ownership of the problem.
- Apology.
- Exceeding expectations – free wine!
- Personalised service.
- Speed of response.
- Positive attitude.
- No blaming of systems.

EXERCISE

Now think of a specific time when you were satisfied with the service you received. The experience could be in retail, restaurants, hotels, travel, etc. How did you feel? What factors contributed to your satisfaction? Try to separate the experience itself from the factors that caused you to feel the service exceeded your expectations.

List the factors that contributed to your satisfaction.

We will return to these ideas when we have described in more detail the two types of service.

MATERIAL AND PERSONAL SERVICE

There are two types of service: material and personal.

Defining material service

Material service, or the content part of service, consists of price, timing, quality and quantity of:

- equipment
- products
- physical comfort
- delivery
- procedures
- routines
- staffing
- information
- definition of roles and responsibilities.

Material service relates to the tangible parts of the service delivery process. For retail organisations the material service is comprised of the storefront, display cases, inventory, cash registers, product information, etc.

EXERCISE

If you are in the service delivery business, what are the material service aspects of your product?

Defining personal service

Personal service consists of the interpersonal aspects in providing service, which include:

- body language
- verbal communication
- using the customer's name
- giving your undivided attention
- showing respect for the individual
- being calm and confident.

Personal service relates to the intangible aspects of providing your product or service. These are harder to measure, control and manage because they take place at the moment of the interaction, cannot be standardised and vary from one moment to another – personal service is situational.

For retail organisations the personal service comprises the effectiveness of the sales person in establishing rapport, identifying customer needs, suggesting appropriate products and describing them in customer-friendly terms, etc.

EXERCISE

If you are in the service delivery business, what are the personal service aspects of your product?

RESEARCHING MATERIAL AND PERSONAL SERVICE

Material service is the easier to define, measure and compare. When complaints are received or market research conducted, it is more likely that the easily defined points of material service will be commented on.

When Jan Carlzon, the Chief Executive Officer of Scandinavian Airlines (SAS) took over SAS in 1981, the airline was not popular with airline travellers. He conducted market research and found that customers said they wanted the material service of the airline to be improved – bigger planes, more leg room, quicker baggage handling and better food. At the same time he came across research conducted in a library in the US.

The library example: first group

To conduct research two groups were used. For the first group the librarian was told that she was in the book-stamping business, not to be rude but to move the customers through the checkout quickly and efficiently. These customers were interviewed when they left the library. Initially somewhat reluctant to be interviewed, their comments on the service they had received included:

- The library was dark.
- It was hard to find the books.
- The library was unwelcoming.
- Overall they were dissatisfied with the service experience.
- No one mentioned the librarian.

The library example: second group

For the second group the librarian was told to do three things:

1 Use the customer's name – it was on the card, so not a complicated request.

2 Smile – they were told to not be effusive but since it uses more muscles than a frown it's good exercise.

3 Touch the customer's hand as he/she passed the book back. (Due to increasing sensitivity to sexual harassment, we only recommend using the first two).

These customers were also interviewed as they left the library. This group seemed more willing to be interviewed and made the following comments on the service they had received:

- The library was warm.
- The filing system was easy to understand.
- The lighting and ventilation was good.
- Overall they were satisfied with the service experience.
- No one mentioned the librarian.

The library example: conclusions

Although the customers commented on the *material* aspects of the service, the differentiating factor, and the only thing that had changed, was the *personal* service the customers had received.

When Jan Carlzon heard about this research he decided instead of initially investing in new aeroplanes, better food, etc (the material aspects), to invest in training the people in the airline on how to provide personalised service to each customer. He invested in a two-day programme called 'Personal Service through Personal Development' that was offered to all his 12,000 employees. The results, as they say, are history! Passengers started to comment on the improvement in flying SAS, and the consequent increase in credibility and passenger flow enabled Jan Carlzon to invest in some of the more important material aspects of service. This approach was then adopted by British Airways, who also implemented this 'wall-to-wall' training which we will discuss in a later chapter.

EXERCISE

Revisiting the factors that made you satisfied and dissatisfied

Go back to the lists of factors that made you satisfied and those that made you dissatisfied. Mark the factors that represent personal service with a P and material service with an M. Some factors, such as lack of product information, could be a combination of both personal and material factors. Review the list and identify which factors appear most often – personal or material. Most lists have more personal than material service factors.

Material and personal service

To summarise, if material service is up to standard it has, at best, a neutral effect on the customer. In planning their service policies most companies focus on the material aspect of service. The personal aspect is often overlooked.

> Personal service is a key element that contributes to customer satisfaction and long-term customer loyalty.

If a customer receives satisfactory material service, but poor personal service, the service is often described as bad or unsatisfactory. If a customer receives poor material service, but excellent personal service, the service is often perceived as good or satisfactory.

As we move on to deciding how to keep customers, it is important to ensure that material service processes and procedures are adequate and not preventing service providers from meeting customer needs. However a greater emphasis will be placed on how to establish and ensure consistent personal service – the factor that makes or breaks the customer's perception of the service delivered.

INTERNAL AND EXTERNAL SERVICE

Too frequently we think of customer service as an external activity: something that occurs outside the organisation to keep paying customers happy. But internal customer service is equally important.

Internal customer service

Internal customer service is the same as external customer service; it just applies to the people within the company rather than outside it. It means delivering competent, quality work in a courteous and helpful manner for colleagues. We all have customers and we are all customers.

Good internal service is important because:

- Internal customer service instils a spirit of co-operation and teamwork in your organisation. Everyone feels 'This is a great place to work.'

- Internal customer service helps everyone produce top-quality work . . . on time and within budget.

- Internal customer service will help your company, and you, to grow.

- Internal customer service helps you feel better about your job. You'll enjoy what you do even more.

The relationship between good internal and external customer service

Working together, people and departments, is what good internal customer service is about.

Your external customers are only satisfied with the best service and/or product. It's only by working together internally that the best can be achieved. External customer service often mirrors internal customer service.

THE SERVICE PYRAMID

Service delivery requires an alternative organisational structure based on an inverted pyramid, with three levels: service providers, service support and management (see Figure 1).

— Service providers have direct interaction with the customer.

— Service support personnel provide important internal services so that service providers can meet customer needs.

— Management/leaders provide vital support for this service initiative.

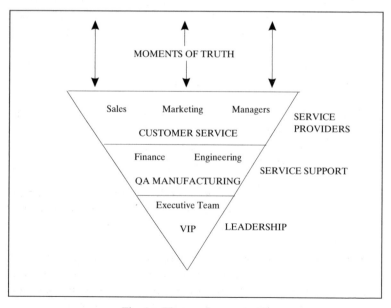

Fig. 1. The service pyramid.

EXERCISE

Who is responsible for helping the customer?

Select a specific customer service transaction that has taken place with your company. Begin with the outcome and then trace the transaction back through the company to identify which are service providers, which are required to support the service and the role of managers in interactions with the customers.

1 Briefly describe the situation.
2 Who were the service providers?
3 Who provided service support?
4 What was the role of managers?

Think about the extent to which each department is focused on meeting customer needs. What internal barriers exist that might prevent service providers from exceeding customer expectations?

CREATING MOMENTS OF TRUTH

The phrase 'moments of truth' represents a powerful idea for helping people in service businesses shift their point of view and think about the customer's experience.

- A moment of truth represents the critical interaction a customer has with an organisation.

Jan Carlzon used the phrase to great effect when he described the airline as having 50,000 moments of truth every day.

Managing service means managing the moments of truth, so that as many as possible turn out positively.

- A moment of truth is any point in the interaction during which the customer has an opportunity to form an impression of the service provided by the company.

Some moments of truth are created by systems – eg no map given of a hotel layout at check-in. Some moments of truth are created by interaction with personnel from the company: asking a question and receiving a complete and thorough answer.

Every moment of truth is not created equal; some have a stronger ability to influence the customer's perception of the service. For instance, if the customer is irate and the problem is resolved to their satisfaction, this moment of truth will be given greater weight by the customer in describing the service experience. Unexpected positive moments of truth will also influence the customer's perception of the service – being greeted with a smile walking through hotel corridors by a hotel employee, the use of their name when leaving a restaurant.

Dull moments of truth
The examples of poor customer service you listed in the exercise earlier in this chapter represent 'dull moments of truth'. These are those critical interactions that leave the customer feeling negative, disappointed, unpleasantly surprised, and therefore dissatisfied with the customer service.

Shining moments of truth
The examples of good customer service represent 'shining moments of truth'. These are those critical interactions that leave the customer feeling positive, enthusiastic, pleasantly surprised, and therefore satisfied with the customer service.

Research has shown that it takes, on average, 12 shining moments of truth to compensate for one dull moment of truth.

SERVICE SUMMARISED
As we have seen, service is more complex than simply being a task completed by a customer service department. Service is:

- To a large extent intangible: it cannot be reproduced as a concrete object and it can vary from one moment to the next.

- Situational: what is positive for one customer one day, and meets their expectations, may be perceived differently by the same customer on another day and fail to meet expectations.

- Difficult to measure: one of the ironies of customer service is that the higher you set expectations by delivering exceptional service, the more the customers expect the next time they deal with you. So you may provide better service than a competitor, but because of differing expectations the customer may be satisfied with the competitor's service but not with yours. (Compare your expectations of a meal in a Little Chef to a meal in the Randolph Hotel, Oxford. A smile would be great service from a Little Chef, but you would expect considerably more from the Randolph Hotel.)

- Subjective: depending on people's awareness of service, standards will vary from one individual to another.

- Influenced by the service provider: if the service provider sets expectations effectively, the customer will probably be satisfied. If the service provider sets expectations ineffectively and fails to meet them, the customer will probably not be satisfied. For instance, if you tell the customer you will call at 3 pm and you call at 5 pm, you have not met customer expectations. If you tell the customer you will call the next day, and you call at 5 pm the same day, you have just exceeded the expectations. The same action, but with a differing set of expectations, produces a different level of customer satisfaction.

Don't over-promise and under-deliver. Make sure you under-promise and over-deliver.

- A component in every product a company makes and distributes: there are no companies that just produce products. Even an organisation such as Amazon.com that sells books over the internet has service components: a 'thank you' e-mail after an order is placed, a reminder about new releases pro-actively sent, etc.

- *Not* provided by a customer service department alone.

In the next chapter we introduce a model based on this definition of service, for improving service delivery.

CHECKLIST

1 Did you complete the customer service quiz?

2 Did you identify the factors that made you satisfied or dissatisfied?

3 Did you define for your business the personal and material aspects of the service you provide?

4 Did you map the internal customer flow within your company?

CASE STUDIES

Let's meet the two companies we will be studying as they implement a customer service improvement strategy in order to try to consistently keep customers coming back.

Who is Kitchen Barn?

Kitchen Barn is a division of a large national speciality retailer which currently uses two distribution channels: mail order and retail stores. Kitchen Barn has been one of four divisions of its parent company ever since it was purchased in 1988. In the past year there has been a push to reposition Kitchen Barn in a different market niche, as a more up-market retailer with larger stores and higher-priced merchandise, including furniture. The parent organisation has always had a reputation for providing good customer service, but the new direction and increased competition in the market place have combined to raise awareness to focus on exceeding customer expectations. We will follow this organisation as it restarts its customer focus campaign.

Who is Internet Express?

Internet Express is a software company providing services on the web. The company was created by the merger of two larger organisations two years ago, and since then has grown to its current size by acquiring five more companies. As a result there was not one unifying culture, but a combination of several different ones. Network Logic had a slower-paced, customer-focused approach, but this had resulted in a long product development cycle and a loss of market status. MacDonald software had a more 'get out and make it happen' culture, with shorter product development cycles and less focus on customer loyalty. Neither culture respected or valued what the other brought to the table. The combination of these two diverse cultures, with the often-hostile cultures of the companies that were taken over, resulted in a somewhat unproductive work environment, and as a result spotty customer service. In this case study we will follow the Vice

President of Technical Support as he integrates several different technical support structures and tries to raise overall service levels to the customer.

ACTION POINTS

1 To what extent have you defined the material and personal service you provide to your external customers? What are the most important facets of your material service? How well do you provide exceptional personal service? How could you improve material and personal service levels?

2 How positive are the interactions between the different departments in your company? What internal barriers exist that might affect customer service levels? Which departments appear customer-focused and which appear product-focused? What could you do to raise internal service levels?

3 How do you identify the most important moments of truth that your team, group, company face every day?

2

Exceeding Customer Expectations

As we saw in the previous chapter many of us have an unclear understanding of what customer service really is. It's not surprising therefore, that when organisations try to raise customer service levels many of their efforts appear unsuccessful. In this chapter we will provide a service management model to show what is required to consistently exceed customer expectations. We will also take some time to show how to evaluate current customer service levels. It's hard to improve if you don't know from whence you started! Finally we will revisit our case studies to show how each company established its service management approach and prioritised its plan of attack.

APPLYING A SERVICE MANAGEMENT MODEL

In order to effectively manage moments of truth, applying a service management model is essential. Based on the model originally developed for British Airways and incorporating a continuous improvement philosophy, the process defines critical activities necessary to ensure consistent excellent service delivery in five specific areas (see Figure 2).

1 Establishing a clear customer service strategy.
2 Ensuring the correct people are in place, with the correct skills to deliver outstanding personal service.
3 Establishing clear material service delivery processes.
4 Improving continuously in terms of process improvement, quality monitoring and recovery.
5 Management playing a key daily part in acting as role models for the delivery of these principles.

By implementing certain important milestones in all five categories, it is possible to optimise the critical moments of truth for both personal and material service in the entire service delivery process.

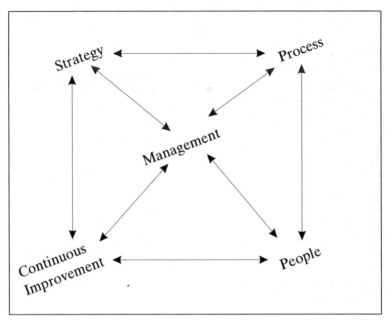

Fig. 2.   The five areas involved in good customer service.

Establishing a customer service strategy

To establish a clear customer service strategy certain key actions are required:

- Understanding the overall organisational vision and mission.

- Defining the organisation's customer service direction.

- Creating the organisation's customer service slogan.

- Establishing the organisation's customer service values.

- Ensuring customer service is defined as a key responsibility for the business/department.

- Sharing the customer service vision via a comprehensive communications programme.

Hiring, training and keeping the right people

Ensuring the right people are in place, with the correct skills to deliver outstanding personal service, requires:

- Hiring the right people.

- Providing training in key areas required to deliver exceptional personal service.

- Providing ongoing coaching and feedback on personal service skills.

- Motivating employees to produce outstanding results.

Managing the material service delivery processes

This critical step involves defining, reviewing and improving service delivery processes and procedures. This requires:

- Mapping the service delivery processes.

- Evaluating critical success points in the process.

- Establishing service delivery procedures to optimise material service.

- Creating service level agreements.

Instituting continuous improvement processes

- Continuous improvement involves reinforcing and adapting both personal and material service delivery processes on an ongoing basis.

- Actions used to reinforce personal service standards are the designing and building of follow-up tools and activities to aid retention.

- Actions used to reinforce material service standards include applying problem-solving to short-term service issues and quality management initiatives.

Manager's role

The key role in the service delivery process is played by the management team, which is responsible for:

- Helping to establish the strategy.

- Understanding the key skills required to deliver outstanding personal and material service.

- Establishing, monitoring and updating service delivery processes.

- Coaching employees in personal and material service delivery skills.

- Acting as an example in delivering outstanding customer service.

We have found that managers play the critical 'make or break' step in the service delivery process.

The rest of this book will concentrate on providing information, skills and tools to be used to establish and maintain effective service delivery processes.

EXERCISE

Assessing your current performance against the model
Answer each question with a number from one to ten as follows:
1 = poor performance in this area
5 = average performance
10 = exceptional performance

Strategy
1 To what extent is your customer service strategy clear?
2 To what extent is your customer service slogan repeated by all?
3 To what extent have you defined your customer service values?
4 To what extent have you communicated your customer service strategy?

People
1 To what extent have you defined the job requirements for service providers?
2 To what extent do you train your people in personal service skills?
3 To what extent do you measure personal service standards?
4 To what extent do you reward exeptional personal service?

Processes
1 To what extent have you defined your material service processes?
2 To what extent do you measure your current performance?

3 To what extent do you define internal service interactions?
4 To what extent have you established service level agreements?

Continuous improvement
1 To what extent have you made it easy for customers to complain?
2 To what extent do you train people how to handle complaints?
3 How effective are you at solving the problem as it happens?
4 How effective are you in looking for the root cause and changing processes as a result of customer complaints?

Managers
1 To what extent are your managers directing the team rather than leading?
2 To what extent do your managers see customer service as part of their job?
3 To what extent do managers coach their staff on personal service skills?
4 To what extent do managers interact with customer?

How did your team rate in each area? Which area do you think needs the most work? Depending on the results of this assessment, you may choose to review chapters 3 to 9 in terms of your priorities rather than follow the sequence of this book:

Chapter 3 Strategy
Chapter 4 People, hiring
Chapter 5 People, developing personal service skills
Chapter 6 People, managing the customer interaction
Chapter 7 Processes, implementing effective processes
Chapter 8 Continuous improvement, dealing with customer complaints
Chapter 9 Continuous improvement processes
Chapter 10 Management/leadership, coaching and motivating employees

ASSESSING YOUR CURRENT CUSTOMER SERVICE

Before an organisation can begin a customer service improvement strategy (unless it's a new company with no history), it's important to identify the current standards in terms of strategy, personal and material service and continuous improvement.

The benefits of defining where you are now include:

- Having a clear starting point in your customer service improvement campaign.

- Being able to measure progress as you institute different approaches.

- Benchmarking your group/function with other similar organisations and groups.

- Gathering more specific data about what the customer actually wants from your company/product/service.

There are several ways to assess the current levels of customer service you are providing:

- customer service questionnaires

- telephone interviews with customers

- focus groups

- face-to-face interviews

- on-line research.

Conducting research in-house

Companies can choose to conduct the research themselves, which has several advantages and disadvantages:

Advantages

- The company has complete access to all data.

- It provides an opportunity to build customer relationships.

Disadvantages

- Designing market research requires specialised expertise.

- Conducting market research is time-consuming.

- There will not be a neutral perspective.

Using specialist researchers

Conversely, using outside companies can have several advantages and disadvantages:

Advantages

- The company gets a neutral, third-party perspective.
- It is less time-consuming for the company.
- An outside provider has existing expertise in designing survey instruments.

Disadvantages

- The consulting organisation may not completely understand your product/service and the information you require.
- You lose the opportunity to communicate directly with your customers.

Companies that can help you conduct customer research include market research organisations, independent consulting firms, firms that focus in a specific market segment (eg Datapro in technical support centre environments) and many new web community site providers such as Talk City.

Specific examples of the differing forms of market research are:

- Customer service questionnaires:
  — to customers to evaluate their service experience, such as Datapro
  — conducting internal attitude surveys to assess employee satisfaction
  — using customer feedback forms.

- Telephone interviews with customers, such as a garage calling after a car has been serviced. This could be internally or externally implemented.

- Focus groups: companies using brainstorming sessions with customers to evaluate new product ideas.

- Face-to-face research:
  — talking to new employees who might have a fresh outlook
  — using secret shopper services (for retail environments).

- On-line research: facilitating a chat about specific products.

EXERCISE

Deciding your approach to conducting customer research

Think about the different ways of surveying customers that we have discussed:

- customer service questionnaires

- telephone interviews

- focus groups

- face-to-face interviews

- on-line research

1 Which approach will you use to discover where are you now?
2 Which approach do you think would gather the most useful data?
3 To what extent will you conduct the research using your staff?
4 What outside providers could provide additional services to you?

UNDERSTANDING YOUR SERVICE CYCLE

The detailed assessment of where you are now can start by understanding your cycle of service for meeting customer needs. What this means is to track examples of your customers' interaction with your company when using its products and services. For instance, if you operate a consulting company, the steps in the service cycle might be as follows:

- Stimulate leads by placing advertisements in journals (material service).

- Design a web page to raise interest (material service).

- Customer calls (material and personal service).

- Customer talks to consultant on the phone (personal service).

- Customer meets consultant (personal service).

- Customer books work and consultant performs said duties (personal service).

- Consultant invoices client (material service).

- Client pays bill (material service).

- Consultant follows up with client to check on quality of service (personal service).

- Consultant sends client regular newsletters (material service).

For each step in this service cycle it is important to assess:

1 How easy is it for the customer to work with us?
2 What could be done to make our systems more customer-friendly?
3 What else could we do to make our service experience more positive?

EXERCISE

Defining your service cycle and assessing current standards of service

What are the main steps in your service delivery cycle? How is the customer introduced to you? What happens next? What are the other important steps?

For each step in this service cycle:

1 How easy is it for the customer to work with you?
2 What could be done to make your systems more customer-friendly?
3 What else could you do to make your service experience more positive?
4 What other services could you add?
5 What processes actually hinder the service delivery at this point?
6 What processes might be added to smooth service delivery at this point?
7 What will you do differently to improve the effectiveness of your service delivery cycle?

CHECKLIST

1 Did you assess your current performance against the customer service model?

2 Did you decide what type of market research you will undertake and who will conduct this research for you?
3 Did you map the steps in your service delivery cycle?

CASE STUDIES

Kitchen Barn: the driving force

Kitchen Barn had hired a new Senior Vice President of retail
in the market place. A new retail organisation had recently
been established and the rapid growth of web-based selling was
challenging their traditional distribution channels. While the
organisation separately decided to investigate more web-based
and catalogue marketing, the Senior VP of Retail, Gary, was
given the task of deciding strategies to protect Kitchen Barn's
position in the retail market. While there are several positioning
possibilities, since Kitchen Barn is a premium price provider,
Gary felt that the most effective direction would be to use the
top-service, premium-priced model for the business.

In the later chapters we will present how he drove the strategy,
instituted a comprehensive training programme, consistently updated procedures, and used reinforcement to keep the initiative
alive and well. With his management team as the main trainers for
the programme they acted as the champions for the process and
were able to coach and reinforce the skills.

Kitchen Barn: where are they now?

Kitchen Barn completed regular secret shopper surveys, conducted by an outside agency, to assess their current levels of
service. These surveys showed clearly that while the personal
service was normally acceptable, customers still perceived the
company products to be overpriced. Also there tended to be an
inconsistency in the way customers were treated. The research
gave valuable foundation data, and was updated as training was
rolled out, when more specific focus areas were identified. In
addition, Gary would spend time with new employees within four
weeks of them joining the organisation, to ask them what they
would change based on their prior experience and their insights in
their first days of employment.

Internet Express: the driving force

Before Internet Express was created by the merger of Network Logic and MacDonald Software, Network Logic was uniquely positioned towards a small, highly technical audience. The people who worked for the organisation were highly-qualified engineers whose customers were similar to them: technically competent and passionate about the product.

As a result of the merger, the company's products were repositioned into more of the enterprise server market and the customer base broadened. Now the customer could be anyone, from the technical-development engineer to the Vice President of Operations or the end user. This meant that the role of the technical support function changed from fixing the problem with a person who was technically literate, to sometimes having to 'fix the customer' in terms of educating and communicating effectively. The customer's agenda could now be anything from needing information, to wanting complex data explained in a simple way, to political manoeuvring.

As a result, the requirements for those who interacted with the customer changed, and individuals needed to become more 'problem managers' rather than 'problem fixers'. Rather than just training the people in personal service skills, the Vice President, Arthur, initiated a complete service development strategy covering the customer service values, changing hiring requirements, instituting service level agreements and changing measurement criteria. More details will be included in later chapters.

Internet Express: where are they now?

Internet Express commissioned a preliminary written customer service survey in order to assess current customer satisfaction levels. This survey indicated that apart from the considerable product issues (such as that the product was unreliable, product upgrades took too long), the staff were perceived as discourteous and unprofessional. This survey provided the base knowledge for the customer service improvement process. In addition, the company initiated a programme, conducted by managers, to call a small percentage of customers within two days of them interacting with the support centre. The purpose of these calls was, first for managers to discover the customer's direct perception of the service received, and second as an opportunity to build customer relationships. The customers selected would normally be from major companies, with whom Internet Express wanted to have a long-term business partnership. The data gathered, although less than the more formal written survey, provided a more in-depth, qualitative perspective of the customer's needs.

ACTION POINTS

1 How clear is your customer service strategy? Is it viable, communicated consistently to all, and practised by senior management? Remembering that any message gets diluted 50 per cent at each passing, what can you do to communicate the strategy, and the commitment to the strategy, to your entire organisation?

2 To what extent are the people you are hiring customer focused? How do you reward them for providing exceptional personal service? How do you train them in customer service skills? What could you do to raise the service abilities of your people?

3 To what extent are your material service standards defined. How effective are your service delivey processes. What could you do to improve these processes?

4 How do you track any problems that arise? How could you incorporate solutions to short-term problems into long-term process improvement?

5 To what extent do managers' 'walk the talk' in delivering exceptional service? How could you raise the effectiveness of your managers in leading the service initiative?

6 To what extent have you conducted, or are you conducting, customer research? Which of the approaches described in this chapter would provide you with the most relevant feedback on your current service levels and customer requirements? What could you do to institute a more formalised customer research policy?

3

Developing a Customer Service Strategy

As we discussed in the last chapter, changing or instituting a customer service culture requires not only senior management commitment, but also a clear and cohesive customer service strategy. In this chapter we will explain and discuss the important steps needed to create this cohesive customer service direction (see Figure 3). These steps include creating a customer service vision and strategy and then assessing the critical competencies and weaknesses in delivering exceptional service as they relate to the customer needs. We also need to define customer service values and ensure that the company, team or group remains focused on an ongoing basis on customer service. Finally we will create a plan to communicate this strategy clearly and consistently to all employees.

INITIATING THE COMPANY VISION STATEMENT

The company's vision statement gives a clear image of where the company wants to be in the future, including the reason for its existence. The purpose of a company's vision statement is to guide daily decision-making in the organisation and capture the essence of what needs to be done in order to succeed. It serves as the guiding philosophy for the organisation and helps to define the way the company operates, focusing attention on the future.

A great example of a vision statement is:

- Ritz Carlton Hotels: 'The Ritz Carlton is a place where genuine care and comfort of our guests is our highest mission.'

When a customer service strategy is initiated, it's important that it is in alignment with the organisation's overall direction as stated in the company vision, otherwise the initiative will not succeed.

DOING A SWOT ANALYSIS

Focusing on customer service, SWOT analysis takes a probing look at the strengths, weaknesses, opportunities and threats that face the company or team in delivering exceptional service. The analysis is a process of investigation and brainstorming the factors working for and against the company that could affect overall service levels. Strengths and weaknesses refer to the company's internal advantages and potential disadvantages. It is important that these factors are in the direct control of the team carrying out the analysis. Opportunities and threats allude to aspects outside the company's direct control that might open up potential (opportunities) or result in negative consequences (threats). Opportunities and threats can originate from outside the company in the market at large, from other organisations, or even from other departments within the company itself.

The purpose of SWOT analysis is to view the world in which you are trying to provide service from the vantage point of the big picture. This ensures that the planned strategy and direction are possible, given the company's inherent strengths and weaknesses. It also assures that the strategy is geared towards capitalising on opportunities and minimising threats.

EXERCISE

Conduct a SWOT analysis for your company for delivering exceptional service. You may want to revisit the exercises you completed in Chapter 2 on defining your service cycle and ways it can be improved.

1 What are your company's **strengths**?
2 What are your company's **weaknesses**?
3 What are your company's **opportunities**?
4 What are your company's **threats**?

CUSTOMER SERVICE STRATEGY

Customer service strategy comes from the company's vision and SWOT analysis.

An effective customer service strategy should meet these requirements:

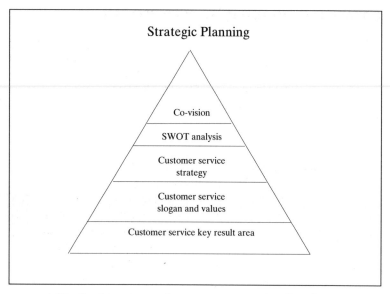

Fig. 3. Steps to creating a customer service direction.

1 It should be developed by the staff.
2 It should be in an easily remembered form.
3 It should set high standards so that accomplishing the strategy means you will be delivering exceptional service.
4 It must have **broad support**. The entire company – management, staff and supporting activities – must 'walk the talk' every day.
5 It must be aligned with the company's vision statement.

The purpose of the customer service strategy is to guide daily decision-making and capture the essence of what customer service needs to be in order to succeed.

Examples:

• Avis Rent-A-Car: 'We're number two, so we try harder.'

• Stew Leonard Groceries: 'Rule #1: The customer is always right. Rule #2: If you think the customer is wrong, read Rule #1.'

CREATING A CUSTOMER SERVICE SLOGAN

The customer service slogan or 'mantra' exists to capture the substance of the customer service strategy in a short phrase. The benefit of this slogan is to focus energy and interest around the customer service strategy. Examples include:

- Nike: 'Just do it.'

- British Airways: 'Put the customer first.'

- Ford: 'Quality is job one.'

Too often organisations create a slogan, but then don't follow through in other areas to manage the service delivery process. For instance, the president of a financial printing company decreed that customer service was a priority for 1998, without understanding how difficult it would be to make his vision a reality. His team, with unclear direction and no senior management commitment, proceeded to undertake a company-wide communications programme, complete with gizmos (cups, T-shirts, etc). The result, as you might have expected, was extra costs, a 'muddy' messge, a perception of 'management flavour of the month', and no difference in customer service levels.

The Ritz Carlton hotel chain has named its customer service philosophy The Gold Standard. It includes:

The Credo:

- We pledge to provide the finest personal service and facilities for our guests who will always enjoy a warm, relaxed yet fine ambience.

- The Ritz Carlton experience enlivens the senses, instils well-being, and fulfils even the unexpressed wishes of our guests.

Slogan

- We are ladies and gentlemen serving ladies and gentlemen.

Three Steps of Service:

1 A warm, sincere greeting. Use the guest name, if and when possible.
2 Anticipation and compliance with guest needs.

3 A fond farewell. Give them a warm goodbye and use their names, if and when possible.

The Twenty Basics:

- Twenty rules for ensuring excellent service.

EXERCISE

1 Write down your company's vision.
2 Write down your company's customer service strategy.
3 Write down your company's customer service slogan.

Think about the following questions with regards to your customer service strategy:

- Is anything written in the company vision statement that might inhibit delivery of exceptional customer service, such as cost management etc?

- Do you have a customer service strategy?

- Is senior management committed to the customer service strategy?

- Is there a customer service slogan?

- Does this slogan have the support and understanding of all people in the company?

- If front-line employees were to be asked, would they be able to repeat this slogan and strategy?

If the answer to many of these questions is no, and your SWOT analysis indicated a different business direction, your chances of instituting a successful customer service culture are relatively small. Your challenge is then to decide:

1 Can you obtain senior management commitment and focus?
2 Do you want to continue to build customer service from the bottom up, almost against the culture of the company?

When organisations decide to institute a customer service culture, more often than not they have to slow down in the short term in order to gain management commitment and produce more effective long-term results.

DEFINING OUR CUSTOMER SERVICE VALUES

When trying to improve performance, whether it is in customer service, quality, or profitability, there are two elements that need to be addressed:

- the task
- and the group process.

The task element relates to anything that needs to be done to achieve the goal and tends to focus on the outcome. The group process element relates to how well people are interacting with each other, to produce the desired results. Both components need to be working well in order to meet objectives.

The customer service strategy and slogan give direction in terms of what the company wants to achieve: the task element in delivering exceptional customer service. It is equally important for companies to establish customer service values. Defining these values is a way of establishing how people in the company are committed to treating each other: the framework for internal customer service. Ultimately these internal values have a direct impact on external customer service levels.

Examples of values are:

- achievement
- communication
- customer comes first
- empowerment
- honesty
- loyalty
- participation
- respect
- sense of humour

- commitment
- co-operation
- empathy
- encouragement
- innovation/creativity
- open-mindedness
- proactiveness and reactiveness
- responsiveness
- service.

EXERCISE

Defining customer service values

1 Select a team made up of individuals from different levels in the company.
2 Individually, consider the values you believe are important to your company in delivering exceptional service. The values may be included on the above list, but they may also be different.
3 As a group, combine the values and agree on the top five you believe will contribute to exceeding customer expectations.

CUSTOMER SERVICE AS A KEY RESULT AREA

Once a company has committed to instituting a customer service culture, this strategy needs to be included as a fundamental focus for the business; this is called a key result area.

What are key result areas?

Establishing key result areas is a valuable technique that links the overall priorities and workload of the company with customer service strategy, project goals and milestones. Key result areas do not describe the type of results to be achieved, but rather categorise work into headings. This grouping procedure is a valuable tool in categorising workload as the process complements the way the human brain naturally works.

Building an overview in the brain

Our brains are structured into three levels of consciousness:

- The **subconscious brain** works 24-hours a day and has, as far as we know, unlimited capacity. The challenge with the subconscious brain is that it runs as a random access device – in other words, it has no filing system from which we can easily call up information.

- We also have a **conscious brain**, which works only when we are awake and can concentrate on only *one thought* at a time. As a result, when we have a multitude of tasks to complete we feel overloaded. However, the third level of the brain, the preconscious, helps us by keeping track of an effective over-view.

- The **preconscious brain** can keep an outline of seven +/- two (ie five to nine categories). If the group can create a list of approximately seven areas of responsibility covering all aspects of their work, they will have a complete overview from which to set realistic goals and milestones. In addition, employees feel more in control and stress levels are reduced when they can see the big picture.

Key result areas

Examples of typical organisational key result areas are:

1 Financial control management
2 Marketing sales
3 Operations
4 People
5 Customer service
6 Manufacturing
7 Distribution
8 Research and development.

EXERCISE

Defining your team/company's key result areas

Conduct this exercise with multiple members from your management team.

1 Individually, on separate stick-on notes, list the specific tasks that you complete on a regular basis: one task per note. Make sure you list as many activities as you can.
2 If you have categories such as e-mail or telephone, be more specific about the purpose of the e-mail: eg are they to customers, to internal departments, etc.
3 When you are individually running out of ideas, start to work in groups of three.
4 As you work together, eliminate the duplicate tasks or activities.
5 Next group these tasks or activities under sample headings,

such as the ones discussed earlier, or choose from the list below.

6 Make sure you use *no more than* seven headings.

7 Make sure customer service is one of these headings or key result areas.

List your company's key result areas. Some sample categories are shown to help you get started with your own.

financial	sales
marketing	team development
customer service	operations
communication	reporting
projects	quality
research and development	manufacturing
vendor management	purchasing
process improvement	problem identification

Is customer service a key result area for your business? If it isn't, it is highly unlikely that you will be able to deliver exceptional service. If it is – great news – move onto the next step! If not, ask again if customer service is really a driving force for your business. If it isn't, don't try to begin a customer service campaign. If you're not committed to it, it will not succeed.

COMMUNICATING THE STRATEGY

Once an organisation has committed to instituting a customer service culture, this strategy and direction needs to be communicated to the entire company. There is only one guideline when trying to announce the strategy: it is communicate, communicate, communicate and then, if in doubt, communicate! You need to balance face-to-face, written and electronic communication channels.

Communication tools and methodologies include:

- Regular newsletters around the theme of the customer service initiative.

- Design of corporate identity around the customer service strategy, so every communication piece has the same look and feel.

- 'Town hall' meetings where the President/CEO holds regular meetings with the company, restating the customer service theme. With today's technology, even global companies can hold these meetings for all locations using video conferencing and satellite links.

- Posters using the slogan.

- Training programmes and seminars.

- E-mail announcements.

- Give-aways such as t-shirts, desk gizmos, pens, paper cutters, etc.

- Contests and awards.

For instance Ritz Carlton introduces all new employees to its Gold Standard programme in an intensive orientation programme. All 14,000 ladies and gentlemen keep this information in sight and in mind using a pocket-sized laminated card. Research with organisations such as Ritz Carlton has shown that it takes approximately two years until this message is received, understood, believed and acted upon within an entire organisation.

CHECKLIST

1 Do you understand your company's vision and mission statement and does it support giving great service to customers?
2 Have you conducted a SWOT analysis for your company?
3 Have you defined your customer service strategy and slogan?
4 Have you defined your customer service values?
5 Have you defined your organisation or group's key result areas?
6 Have you designed a communication plan?

CASE STUDIES

Kitchen Barn: setting the strategy

Kitchen Barn's vision and mission
The core of Kitchen Barn is expressed in their vision: 'We are in the business of enhancing the quality of life at home – helping

people derive greater pleasure and social enjoyment from their home environment through high-quality, well-designed innovative products and exemplary service.' As you can see, customer service is inherently part of this value proposition.

When Gary's drive to improve customer service was compared with these statements and the history of the business, they were found to be in very close alignment. Many of the most successful retail organisations have created their market niche using customer service as the way they differentiate themselves from their competitors.

Kitchen Barn's SWOT analysis
In a strategic planning process with the executive team, they identified the following sample strengths, weaknesses, opporunities and threats as they related specifically to providing exceptional service:

Strengths:

- passion
- humour
- improvisation
- compassion
- commitment
- talent
- organisation
- reputation.

Weaknesses:

- underuse of resources
- systems
- reactive not proactive
- lack of vision/optimism
- unfocused
- lack of punctuality

- no planning.

Opportunities:
- services (interior design)
- direct mail
- involvement in community
- editorial
- new suppliers
- new markets
- advertising
- internet
- promotions/city events
- creating own product
- baby boomers.

Threats
- competition
- bad press
- economy
- disloyalty
- managing supply chain
- market saturation
- vendors
- lack of integrity

Despite what appeared to be a clear vision and mission statement, the customer service message did not appear to be understood on the shop floor. This confused the executive team who thought this was understood by all working for Kitchen Barn. As a result, they realised that the customer service focus would benefit from a slogan and clearer communication with the people on the front line.

Creating a customer service strategy
Gary decided to restate the importance of customer service to Kitchen Barn by saying the strategy was: 'To provide the best customer service in the housewares industry in order to maximise customer satisfaction and retention.'

Creating a customer service slogan
From this high-level strategy statement, the slogan for Kitchen Barn became: 'To make every customer feel like an honoured *guest* in our stores.'

The combination of the strategy statement and the slogan would act as the foundation for the rest of the service management programme.

Customer service values
The team of district managers completed the values exercise in this chapter to clarify the customer service values for the retail organisation. When the results were collated, it showed that the team had agreed upon a cohesive set of values:

- respect

- honesty

- sense of humour

- creativity

- commitment.

Customer service as a key result area
Kitchen Barn defined its key result areas as follows:

1 Customer service
2 Marketing
3 Sales
4 Merchandising
5 Inventory management
6 Operations
7 People/morale
8 Financial management.

Under the customer service key result area, the team highlighted possible programmes such as:

- creating a clientele book system
- special orders
- wedding registry
- personal shopping.

More specific tasks and activities to support this strategy and formalise these ideas will be described in later chapters.

Communicating the customer service strategy
As the SWOT analysis had revealed, all associates did not have a clear understanding of the customer service strategy. Gary refocused his communications around customer service in the following way:

- He sent out a letter to all staff describing the strategy and slogan and explaining the reason for this direction.
- He went to every store during the pre-Christmas roll-out to personally communicate with as many staff members as possible the importance of customer service.
- He initiated and supported a 'wall-to-wall' training programme (see Chapter 5).
- He produced a logo for a 'guest' approach to the way customers were treated.
- His retail operations team created a monthly guest update newsletter.
- He started special rewards and recognition programmes to support the strategy (see Chapter 10).
- He initiated a weekly conference call with all 20 district managers, where the first agenda item was customer service: sharing success stories and ideas for improvement.
- Not only did he communicate within his division, but with the rest of the organisation about the customer service focus.

Internet Express: setting the strategy
Arthur decided to hold several off-site meetings with his direct and extended management team to set a cohesive customer

service strategy. His approach was hard to implement consistently because of the overall vision and culture of the company.

Internet Express vision and mission

Internet Express had a vision that had guided the strategic direction of the organisation in the five years of its existence and differing company names. This statement was: 'To be the world-wide leader in enterprise software for distributed-computing enterprise environments.'

Obviously customer service plays an important role in becoming a world-wide leader in any specific field. However, in the software industry having the most current, technologically advanced products also heavily influences market leadership. Sometimes these drives are at odds. For instance, the organisation may be pressured to release a new product to remain in a market leadership position. However, if this product has not been adequately tested, it may create customer dissatisfaction and complaints. The technical support function is in a critical position in maintaining long-term loyalty, but also has limited control over release dates for new products. Despite this apparent lack of alignment, Arthur decided to proceed with his customer service strategy as he felt the market required them to be more customer focused.

Internet Express SWOT analysis

Taken from a management retreat, the following represents a cross-section of the types of ideas that the team identified:

Strengths

- Commitment.
- Enthusiastic team.
- Strong visionary leadership.
- Organisation structure now integrated from multiple support structures to three support centres.

Weaknesses:

- Lack of processes and procedures.
- New company so no 'history' to refer to.

- Geographically dispersed (three centres world-wide).
- Relatively young, inexperienced management team.

Opportunities:

- Build a name for customer service.
- Lots of market growth with the expansion of the internet.
- Ability to create own format and structure.
- CEO who believes in the value of technical support.

Threats:

- Lack of communication/co-ordination between engineering (who develop the product) and technical support.
- If the product is unreliable it strains resources.
- Different physical location from headquarters – out of sight/ out of mind.
- Other competitors entering the market and providing better service.

Arthur decided he would define his customer service strategy to capitalise on the strengths and opportunities, and that he would try to identify specific tactics to minimise weaknesses and reduce threats. He felt that customer service in today's technical world was non-negotiable, and that money and time invested in this area was as important as investment in new tools and technologies.

Internet Express strategy and slogan
The strategy that was decided for the technical support group was to move from a 'drive fast, take chances' mentality to a 'treat the customer as you would wish to be treated' culture. He felt that this strategy included both internal and external customers, and captured the important meaning behind a customer-focused approach. 'The purpose of World-wide Support Services is to maximise customer retention.'

The slogan the team chose was: 'One team, one centre, the best solution.'

This slogan was meant to unite the three teams, and the various levels of support (front line level one, back line level two and product support level three). It also focused on the solutions aspect of meeting customer needs.

Internet Express values
The group decided to adhere to the company values that were clearly defined and located on posters, business cards, etc. The team thought that changing these values might cause confusion for the engineers and appear to not be aligned with the overall corporate direction. Samples of these corporate values were:

- Do the right things – don't just do things right.

- The only constant is change.

- Treat others as you wish to be treated.

Customer service as a key result area
Internet Express defined its key result areas as follows:

1 Customer service
2 Problem resolution
3 Process re-engineering
4 People management
5 Research and development
6 People
7 Financial requirements
8 Internal communication
9 Marketing service contracts.

A technical support department should always have a customer service key results area.

Communicating the Internet Express strategy
Arthur used various techniques to communicate the customer service strategy:

- He held all-hands meetings at the three support centres.

- He distributed via e-mail his overal goals for the upcoming year, which showed a strong emphasis on customer satisfaction.

- He instituted a high achievers award for those who had demonstrated exceptional service skills (see Chapter 10).

- He held regular meetings with those who reported directly to him where they discussed customer success stories.

- He regularly published any positive customer feedback.

- He created screen-savers with the slogan and strategy.

- He introduced a skills-enhancement training programme for everyone who had contact with customers (see Chapter 6).

ACTION POINTS

1 To what extent is your corporate vision statement in alignment with instituting a customer service strategy? What will you do if customer service is not supported by the corporate vision statement?

2 When you conducted the SWOT analysis, what organisational factors were strengths in providing exceptional customer service and which were limitations? What factors existed outside of the organisation that would necessitate and support a customer service imperative, and which would possibly inhibit its implementation? How will you use this data to improve service effectiveness?

3 Based on the answers to questions 1 and 2, is a customer service strategy realistic and feasible at this time? What is the main business driver? Is senior management committed to customer service or are they paying lip service to the idea? How could the service direction be made a reality?

4 If the answers to question 3 are positive, what steps will you take to decide the most important customer service values?

5 How will you implement customer service as a key result area?

6 How will you start the internal communications campaign? How will you use face-to-face, e-mail and written communication? How will you ensure that communication is ongoing and consistent in terms of message and delivery?

4

Recruiting the Right People

In order to consistently exceed customer expectations, we need not only a clear strategy but to find the right people, with the critical skills required to provide exceptional service. In this chapter we discuss how to manage the recruitment process to identify and meet the specific requirements for the job. The recruitment process involves more than just placing an advertisement! Then we look at specific interviewing strategies to ensure we select the right people, those with a customer focus. Finally we reveal how our companies in the case studies were able to hire the right people for their teams. With the best will in the world, if you hire the wrong people any customer service programme will not succeed: 'It's really hard to teach an elephant to dance!'

EMPLOYING OR TRAINING CUSTOMER SERVICE SKILLS

When recruiting employees to provide customer service, the process often tends to concentrate more on skills, functional expertise, technical competence and knowledge than on inter-personal skills. However, lack of a positive customer service attitude can drastically impact customer service levels.

> The CEO of a high-tech company was in a cab in London with his Vice President of Sales. They were debating the critical competencies for sales people. He believed it was better to recruit people with the correct interpersonal skills/customer focus, and then provide them with technical training. His VP of Sales believed strongly that sales people should first have technical knowledge, and later develop the interpersonal and selling skills. The cab driver interrupted their debate and asked if he could act as the guinea pig. He had interpersonal and relationship building skills, but absolutely no technical knowledge. He joined the company, and within five years became the number one sales person.

The message is this: when considering hiring people in roles where they need functional knowledge and interpersonal skills, it is better to hire the interpersonal skills and train the technical side rather than vice versa.

MANAGING THE RECRUITMENT PROCESS

The recruitment process is made up of several important steps:

- Defining individual job requirements.

- Sourcing candidates.

- Reviewing background information.

- Creating interview questions.

- Conducting telephone screening.

Let's take a more detailed look at each of the steps within the recruitment process.

Defining individual job requirements

When hiring service providers, it's your responsibility to ensure that the person you hire is capable of doing the job as defined by the job description. Therefore, once a job description has been developed, specific job requirements should be identified for each position.

Job requirements are the required and desired qualities that are necessary for success on the job. Job requirements include:

- education

- work/related experience

- skills and knowledge

- job characteristics (the most important job requirements are the job characteristics).

One tool that will help you evaluate applicants is a job requirements checklist. Below are some job dimensions that you can use to create your own checklist.

Characteristics/job dimensions

Communications:

- oral communication
- written communication
- listening.

Personal/motivational:

- work standards
- self-organisation
- initiative
- attention to detail
- patience.

Interpersonal influence:

- assertiveness
- leadership
- persistence
- persuasiveness/sales ability
- flexibility
- versatility
- team orientation
- responsiveness.

Management:

- planning and organising
- delegation.

Problem-solving/decision making:

- analysis
- creativity

- logic
- judgement
- decisiveness
- risk-taking.

EXERCISE

Building individual job requirements

1 Think about a particular service provider role.
2 Define the major responsibilities for that role.
3 Then define the job dimensions that are important for this job role.
4 Pay particular attention to selecting the critical job characteristics for that role. Try to limit these to four.

Sourcing candidates

The purpose of a sourcing strategy is to increase the quality and quantity of the pool of candidates available to you to screen and interview. Depending on the size of your company, it is possible to source candidates both internally and externally.

Internal sourcing
Internal sourcing involves placing a job posting internally to identify potential candidates who are in other departments in the company. Most organisations have an internal recruitment policy, and human resources can normally provide details of this process.

External sourcing
There is a wide variety of sourcing channels open to you when trying to hire externally. These include:

- **Unsolicited CVs**: sent by applicants who have targeted your company.

- **Advertising**: an extremely cost-effective way to source candidates if managed correctly. It can include newspapers, both local and regional, internet, association newsletters (in your field), radio, magazines, university job listings, etc.

Whichever medium you select the advertisement must be written to clearly describe the job requirements you identified earlier. Often companies have arrangements with specific agencies that help to put together and place recruitment advertising.

- **Recruitment agencies/search firms**: there are two types of recruitment agencies – retainer and contingency—
   —retainer firms are retained by the company to locate qualified candidates for specific positions. They are paid a standard fee by the company regardless of whether the candidates are hired.
   —contingency firms are paid a fee only when a candidate presented by the contingency firm is hired.

- **Web site**: creating a page on your web site listing current job openings.

- **Recruiters**: contract recruiters can be used on an hourly basis.

- **Networking/employee referrals**: one of the best sources of candidates is through word-of-mouth. This process can be maximised by:
   —networking with other managers to share information about openings
   —talking to and e-mailing current employees in case they know a good candidate
   —talking to previous employees
   —checking with your HR manager
   —providing cash rewards for internal referrals
   —keeping your eyes open for great service providers when you are a customer with other organisations. Remember you can train technical skills if you find someone with inter-personal skills.

- **Colleges/universities and internships**: many organisations run extensive campus recruitment campaigns, often managed by the director of recruitment.

- **Associations/professional organisations/user groups/con-ferences**: increasingly, professional organisations can be an excellent source of candidates, particularly if there is specific technical knowledge required – just watch for the interpersonal skills too.

Make sure you use as many sources as you can when recruiting for your team.

EXERCISE

Sourcing candidates
Think of a position you might need to fill for your team.
What sourcing channels could you use?

- unsolicited CVs

- advertising

- recruitment agencies/search firms

- web site

- recruiters

- networking/employee referrals

- colleges/universities and internships

- associations/professional organisations/user groups/ conferences

Reviewing background information
Prior to the interview, the basic written tool available to you will be the CV and/or the application form. The CV is the key document for outside applicants.

Information 'red flags'
The first step in reviewing this written documentation is to identify any information that is incomplete or confusing to you. To clarify your understanding, you will want to ask the applicant about these items prior to the beginning of your face-to-face interview.

Red flags on the written material are:

- Preference for a job that is not presently available.

- Incomplete information, such as missing phone numbers, street addresses, postal codes.

- Stated salary requirements clearly not within the guidelines of the open position.

- Gaps in work or education history.

- Lack of career progress.

Creating interview questions

The way we gather data about a candidate's capabilities is to ask a question about the job requirements. To ensure diversity of questions, and to help gather the information required, it's normally a good idea to prepare interview questions in advance. In the following list one example of an open-ended question is given for each job requirement category.

Job requirements/questions		
Communication	Oral communication	• What different approaches do you use when talking with different people? How do you know you are getting your point across?
	Written communication	• What are some of the most important reports you've written? What reactions did they get? Were they hard to write? Why?
	Listening	• Give some examples from your past jobs when you had to rely on information given to you orally to get the job done.
Personal motivation	Work standards	• Compare and contrast the times when you did work which was above standard and times it was below standard.

	Self-organisation	• What do you do when your time schedule is upset by unforseen circumstances? Give examples.
	Initiative	• What changes have you tried to implement in your area of responsibility? What have you done to get them started?
	Attention to detail	• We've all had times when we just couldn't get everything done on time. When and why has this happened to you?
	Patience	• Give an example of when you had to wait for an important decision or piece of information. How did that affect you?
Interpersonal influence	Assertiveness	• Describe a recent time when you had to deal with an angry or impatient person. What did you do? How did they react?
	Leadership	• Tell me about a new policy or idea you recently implemented which was considerably different from standard procedure. What approach did you take to get your employees to go along with it?
	Persistence	• What are some big obstacles you have had to overcome to get where you are today? How did you overcome them?

	Persuasiveness/ sales ability	• What are some of the best ideas you tried but failed to sell to a superior/peer/ subordinate? What was your approach? Why did they fail?
	Flexibility/ versatility	• Describe a situation when you were required to work with someone you disliked.
	Team orientation	• Tell me about a time when you had difficulty getting others to establish a common approach to a problem. What did you do? What was the outcome?
	Responsiveness	• Describe a situation when you were too late in your response. What did you do?
Management	Planning and organising	• What is your procedure for keeping track of items needing your attention?
	Delegation	• Who is 'minding the store' while you are here? How were they selected? Why? How will you know how they performed?
Problem solving/ decision	Analysis	• Describe the biggest problems you've faced in the last six months. How did you handle them?
	Creativity	• What has been the most creative accomplishment in your current job?

Logic	• Tell me about a complex decision you recently had to make. What were the key elements to consider? How did you make your decision? What was the outcome?
Decisiveness	• How have you made important decisions affecting your career?
Risk-taking	• Tell me about the riskiest management decision you've made (present/ previous company). How long did it take to gather the information to make the decision? How long after that to make the decision? What were the results?

Conducting telephone screening

The telephone is an extremely cost-effective and time-efficient tool in the recruitment and selection process to narrow down the pool of candidates and determine further interest from a candidate.

Guidelines

• Be sure to have the job requirements checklist handy.

• Prepare a list of questions.

• Move through the questions, listening.

• Have a telephone screening form to jot down any notes.

• Select questions based on top-priority job requirements.

• Check availability, compensation requirements, interest, and relocation status (if appropriate).

CONDUCTING THE INTERVIEW

The next step in hiring the right candidates is understanding how to conduct an interview.

The interview process includes the following steps:

- opening the interview
- collecting information from the candidate
- providing information
- closing the interview
- evaluating the candidate.

1 Opening the interview

There are four steps you should follow to open the interview.

(a) create a relaxed atmosphere
(b) explain the interview process
(c) clarify missing or confusing information from CV
(d) give brief information about the company and the position.

2 Collecting information from the candidate

This is the most important part of the interview. Too often, inexperienced interviewers talk about the company and the position instead of collecting as much data as possible from the candidate.

There are eight basic techniques used to collect and confirm information. Many of these techniques are also used to manage the customer interaction and will be described in more detail in Chapter 6.

(a) Open-ended questions

Open-ended questions are questions asked to learn more about the applicant. They begin with such words/phrases as: who, what, where, when, why, how, tell me about . . . , describe . . . , in what way . . . , etc.

(b) Probing for specifics

You have used the opening questions to identify specific job requirements. Now you ask further questions to gather more data in a specific category. For instance, if a candidate said 'In my last job there were always irate customers calling' you could probe for specifics with such questions as 'Tell me about a specific irate customer situation, what did you do in that situation?' etc.

(c) Active listening
The aim of active listening is to focus entirely on the candidate and be aware of content and the underlying meaning being expressed. It is important to separate your listening from the evaluation process.

(d) Paraphrasing
Paraphrasing is restating in your own words what the other person has said. The simplest way to paraphrase is to listen without interrupting, and then follow up with a sentence such as 'So, what you're saying is . . .' Paraphrasing enables you to determine whether or not you have accurately understood the applicant.

(e) Closed questions
Closed questions are used in the interview to verify data, limit an applicant's answer and move from one discussion to another.

(f) Rapport
Uses words and phrases such as 'Oh? I understand, uh huh, of course, interesting' to encourage the applicant to open up.

We also build rapport by mirroring body language, pace and tone.

(g) Silence
Silence in the interview allows the applicant to gather and formulate thoughts, while at the same time giving them an opportunity to respond.

(h) Note-taking
Note-taking in the interview will help you remember, retain focus and provide a useful written record when evaluating the candidate.

3 Providing information and answering questions
When you are satisfied you have gathered all the information you need from the applicant, be prepared to answer questions relating to:

- the job

- the company

- the working environment.

4 Closing the interview

There are two basic steps to closing an interview:

- First explain the steps that follow:
  —review the hiring process
  —tell the applicant what will happen next
  —tell the applicant how and when he/she will be notified of the hiring decision.

- Second, thank the applicant for his/her co-operation and interest in the company. You want to try to remain as neutral as possible and not give the applicant any false encouragement nor negative feedback. Remember that no matter what your final hiring decision may be, the applicant could be a current or potential customer. Be nice.

EXERCISE

Conducting the interview

1 Review the job requirements checklist you prepared earlier.
2 Pick one specific job aspect/characteristic that is critical for your team members to have in order to provide exceptional customer service.
3 Conduct a mini-interview to gather information from a partner to assess his/her competence in this area.
4 Remember to:

- ask open-ended questions

- probe for specifics

- listen actively

- paraphrase

- use closed questions

- use rapport

- use silence

- write notes

5 Debrief with your partner to discuss what you could have done more effectively.

---

5 Evaluating the applicant

Once the interview is complete, it's time to evaluate the applicant and the information you have gathered. If at all possible, it's best to evaluate immediately following the interview. Do avoid evaluation while the interview is in progress: forming opinions and making judgements during the interview itself may lead you to ask only questions that confirm your feeling or hypothesis.

While conducting the evaluation, refer to the job requirements checklist to further validate the information you received during the interview.

Evaluation pitfalls
There are several major pitfalls to be avoided when evaluating the information you receive from an applicant.

- Bias. Try to be aware of any attitudes, prejudices or personal feelings held towards certain groups of people.

- First impressions. Contrary to conventional wisdom, don't go on *initial* gut feelings. More often than not this will lead to a tendency to 'over-test' your hypothesis and ask leading questions that will not provide accurate evidence.

- Mirror image. Just as bias and snap judgements can cause you to evaluate an applicant negatively, the mirror-image pitfall can have exactly the opposite effect. By mirror image we mean the transference of your own self-image onto another person. We all have a tendency to gravitate towards people with tastes and opinions similar to our own. In the interviewing process this tendency might result in evaluating an applicant more favourably than the facts warrant.

Inappropriate information
When evaluating an applicant you will use two sources of information:

1 Information actually reported by the applicant.
2 Observations you made of the applicant's behaviour during the interview.

Remember the information is valid only if it relates to specific job requirements. Do not use information that is irrelevant to successful job performance or that is drawn from a conclusion that cannot be backed up with facts.

Here is an example of appropriate and inappropriate back up information:

Appropriate:
The applicant found it difficult to make decisive answers. They didn't know what they liked or disliked about previous jobs, didn't know whether or not to go back to university, stay in retailing or move into direct sales.

Inappropriate:
Applicant seemed wishy-washy.

The next step
When you have selected the candidate you think is the best fit, you're ready to include that person in your customer service culture through training, a clear orientation to the company, and by providing rewards and recognition to enhance individual performance. We will be looking at these subjects in a later chapter, but let's look at how the companies in our case studies ensured they hired the right people.

CHECKLIST

1 Have you created a job requirements checklist for key service roles?
2 Have you evaluated and selected different sourcing channels?
3 Have you created open-ended questions within each of these categories?
4 Do you telephone-screen candidates?
5 Do you spend more time in the interview asking questions rather than talking about the company and the position?
6 Do you make sure you evaluate the candidate *after* the interview, not during it.

CASE STUDIES

Kitchen Barn: hiring the right people

Kitchen Barn had always used a clear job description when hiring sales associates, and had customised the job requirements form for their audience.

Because of the change in business focus, they realised they needed to create a new position, a product expert, to act as an adviser in each store on the furniture and furnishings questions. Part of the job requirements checklist is given below.

Job requirements checklist
Position: Product Expert
Major responsibilities (from job description)

- Act as adviser to store personnel on measuring and installing curtains and purchasing furniture.

- Organise literature to support questions.

- Other responsibilities were the same as sales associates, ie operating the till, working on the shop floor, inventory management, etc.

Job dimensions (desired/required):

- Education
  —Bachelors Degree desired

- Work experience
  —time spent as an interior designer required
  —work in some sort of furniture/furnishings industry, preferably on the consumer side

- Skills and knowledge
  —knowledge of the furniture industry
  —interior design skills

- Job characteristics
  —communication
  —customer orientation
  —initiative
  —listening
  —organisation
  —team player.

While the focus of this job was definitely more technical, the job requirements checklist ensured that technical competence was not substituted for interpersonal/service skills.

Managing the interview process

The team discovered that by allocating questions to different team members they were able to hold more productive interviews, and to more effectively contrast the answers from various candidates.

Criteria	Ratings 1 = Excellent 10 = Poor	Reason/Notes
Communication		
Customer orientation		
Initiative		
Listening		
Organisation skills		
Team player		
Accountability		

They created an interview evaluation form (shown above) where they rated each candidate against the criteria with a brief explanation as to their rationale for the rating. They met immediately after each interview so that the ideas were fresh in their minds, and charted the composite score for each candidate. They discussed any discrepancies and always placed a greater emphasis on the customer service and communication skills in the final hiring decision. They made a point of questioning whether their rationale for rating each candidate was objective. The group discussion helped to eliminate some of the inherent bias in the evaluation process.

To reinforce the importance of selecting the correct people, Gary invested in training all the district managers in behavioural interviewing at the store managers annual conference.

Internet Express: hiring the right people

Arthur felt that individuals in this area of work tended to be more technical, could 'talk a good line' in the interview, but tended to demonstrate arrogance when interacting with the customer.

For this reason he decided to use an assessment centre, to complement the behavioural interviewing approach that was described in this chapter.

Running an assessment centre involves creating scenarios that future employees might face in the world of work and then allowing them to role-play how they would respond in each situation. Assessment centres tend to avoid some verbal camouflage that abounds in interviews. Have you ever interviewed someone and been really impressed, but then when they start you wonder how you could have been so wrong?

Some of the scenarios presented at the assessment centre were:

- Instructing a really non-technical customer how to install a piece of software (this can cause technical people to get impatient).

- Posing a problem that, although not complex, required several questions for an effective analysis (to assess to what extent the engineer was making assumptions).

- Describing a scenario with multiple agendas (to assess whether the engineer was only in 'fix it' mode).

The result from this approach was that some really top-flight technical applicants were not hired, due to their approach with the customer, and some less seasoned but willing applicants were hired instead.

ACTION POINTS

1 What job requirements have you identified as desired and required for your service providers? How could you formalise the use of these job requirements in your hiring process?

2 When it comes to recruiting people, what other sources of applicants will you investigate. What are some new pools of talent that have the right skill mix, but are not necessarily in

your industry? What untraditional approaches will you use to find new candidates?

3 How else could you use telephoning screening in your hiring process? How could you screen out some of the unsuitable candidates before they are face-to-face with you?

4 What is your current interviewing process? What could you do to raise the competence of those who interview?

5 How many questions have you created to use in the interview? How could you create scenarios and then use the assessment centre approach?

6 How effective are you at evaluating the candidate? What else could you do to avoid the evaluation pitfalls of making decisions too quickly and not using appropriate information?

5

Developing Personal Service Skills

Delivering consistent exceptional personal service is a great challenge to service organisations because personal service is situational. It varies from one moment to the next and from one customer to the next. It also varies for the same customer at different times. This chapter will focus on the communication process and its effect on personal service, describing in some detail the attitude, words, delivery and body language we must use to communicate effectively with customers. In the next chapter we demonstrate how we use other skills to manage the customer interaction, in order to set expectations correctly. Although many of the principles and techniques described in this chapter may seem to be nothing more than common sense, as we all know common sense is not necessarily common practice!

UNDERSTANDING COMMUNICATION

Communication is the exchange of information between sender and receiver. Too often communication is perceived as 'sending an e-mail' or talking to a customer. But in order for communication to be effective, the message must be clear and the receiver must receive it, process and act on it. Communication skills will always require attention and refinement.

THE COMMUNICATION PROCESS

The communication process begins when the sender has an idea, thought or information that they wish to communicate. The sender then must formulate or organise the information considering not only who will be the receiver, but what they wish to achieve as a result of sending the message. When the information has been mentally prepared, it is ready to be sent.

When we are communicating with people face-to-face, we use both verbal and non-verbal communication.

- Verbal communication refers to the actual **words we use** (word choice/dialogue) and the **way we say the words** (tone, pitch and volume).

- Non-verbal communication refers to **body language** (expressions, gestures and posture).

When we communicate with someone with whom we have an ongoing relationship, credibility also plays a role. Credibility usually comes from the amount of connection, knowledge or reliability we recognise in the communicator. The statistics below show that on a first meeting body language is the main component of communication. When we have known someone for a while, credibility becomes more important.

	Initial meeting[1]	Ongoing Meetings[2]
Words we use:	7%	7%
Way we say the words:	38%	14%
Body language:	55%	24%
Credibility:		55%

When we send a message, if we're lucky the other person will receive it. However, too often filters such as bias, insufficient interest, rehearsing, lack of understanding and distraction prevent the listener from receiving the message. If the listener does receive the message, they then process it against their own reference bank and decode it appropriately in order to take action or provide a response.

GETTING THE WRONG MESSAGE

Figure 4 represents a simple explanation of the communication process. All the steps actually happen simultaneously. As the sender is thinking of an idea, they are formulating a sentence and possibly already sending the message. On the other end the receiver is sending back a complex combination of responses

[1]Statistics: Mahrabian
[2]Statistics: Birdwhistle

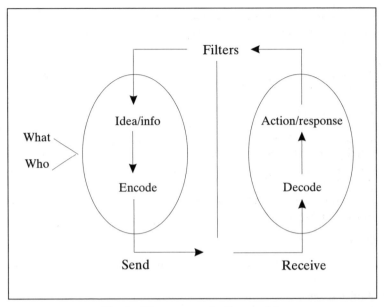

Fig. 4. The communication model.

during the whole transmission, while at the same time processing and decoding the information.

Lots of things can go wrong with the communicating process. The sender may have an irrational idea, want to communicate incorrect data, or formulate the information erroneously for the receiver. By using the wrong words (too complex, too simple, jargon, slang) the sender could also offend, confuse, irritate or bore the receiver. In addition, he/she might not deliver the words effectively (unclear enunciation, inappropriate body language). From the other side the receiver might filter out the message or interpret it incorrectly because of their different frame of reference. The receiver could also provide a completely inappropriate response. The process is so complex that it is amazing anything is communicated accurately at all!

To complicate the process, cultural and individual diversity also contribute to communication confusion. Since many of us come from different countries and ethnic groups, our cultural values and language proficiencies can cause language barriers, misunderstandings and misinterpretations.

Let's look at some guidelines for improving the way we send the message when communicating with customers.

SENDING THE MESSAGE

The words we use

While the actual words used represent only seven per cent of the communication process, word choice is still something to carefully consider. Jargon, complex words and slang can all confuse the receiver, while language that is too simple can be patronising. Some important points to remember about word choice are as follows.

General guidelines

- Be careful with the word 'but': it tends to disqualify all other words used previously in the sentence. For instance 'I am sorry *but* we are busy' negates the apology.

- Use positive words such as: 'We can, we will, let's'.

- Watch 'red flag' words. These are words or phrases that cause a negative reaction with the customer. For instance: 'No, our policy is . . . it's not my job, I don't know.'

- Instead say: 'Normally we . . . I will find out.'

- Use 'we' not 'you' and 'I'.

- Use action words when resolving issues such as: 'Let's get to the bottom of this, let's work towards closure.'

- Don't swear and remember one person's definition of jargon could be the other's definition of swearing.

- Don't use too many words. Keep it simple and precise.

Use of humour

- Be very careful when using humour with customers, particularly if there are problems or issues. Half-laughing and saying things such as 'Dear, dear, this is the third time the machine is down this week – not a good week' could escalate an already stressful customer situation into severe conflict.

- On the other hand, the use of appropriate humour can dissipate negative energy and connect disparate viewpoints. It is best to allow the customer to initiate the humour and to mirror the customer's style.

- Humour is also easier to use when there is an ongoing relationship.

During the interaction

- Be polite and respectful using words such as 'sir', 'Mrs . . .' Wait for permission to use the first name.

- Spell out names and repeat numbers.

- Use the customer's name two to three times during the interaction, particularly at important moments of truth.

Technical terms

- Try to avoid jargon or slang.

- If you use technical terms, make sure you define them.

- Don't make assumptions when talking to those with less technical or product knowledge.

EXERCISE

For your business, list any of the words that might confuse your customers: jargon, red-flag words, acronyms, etc.

The way we say the words

The way we say the words, or the delivery, has a critical impact on the extent to which the message is received accurately. Here are some guidelines to improve the delivery of your message:

- Include some variety in pitch and inflection to add interest to the message. A monotone can cause customers to lose interest quickly!

- Ensure your voice has good tone by using deep breathing and relaxation techniques to give it a stronger, more resonant quality.

- The volume of your voice needs to be loud enough for people to hear, but not so loud that it dominates or intimidates. Volume can be adjusted to make important points.

- Speaking quickly may result in the message not being received in its entirety. Speaking slowly may lose the receiver out of boredom. Slow down your rate of speech when providing important information such as detailed instructions or content facts. Quicken your speech pattern when dealing with more routine data.

- Faulty pronounciation, including names, can result in the message not being received accurately. While the listener is trying to interpret the words, they may miss the message. Failing to articulate words clearly may also result in miscommunication. Proper enunciation means keeping your speech clear, precise and easy to listen to.

- We all have bad habits and use filler words such as like, um, you know, uh, etc. These words clutter communication and result in the receiver turning off or even counting the number of filler words we use! Either way, they are not listening any more. So avoid filler words.

- Other guidelines:
  —don't be condescending or judgemental
  —don't sound apathetic or anxious
  —don't get impatient
  —be enthusiastic and encouraging
  —be sincere and genuine
  —do sound caring
  —do sound as if you are calm and in control.

EXERCISE

Delivery

1 Repeat the following sentence several times: 'I did not say you stole the watch.'
2 As you repeat the sentence, place a different emphasis on each word as underlined.
3 Make a note of the different meaning you inferred from the emphasis and why.

(a) **I** did not say you stole the watch
(b) I **did not** say you stole the watch
(c) I did not **say** you stole the watch
(d) I did not say **you** stole the watch
(e) I did not say you **stole** the watch
(f) I did not say you stole **the** watch
(g) I did not say you stole the **watch**.

Answers for these interpretations are given below.

As you can see, changing only the emphasis changed the whole meaning of the sentence. Getting upset or stressed can cause us to change our delivery, inadvertently influencing the receiver in a negative way.

Answers
(a) Someone else said you stole it
(b) Firm emphasis
(c) I inferred you stole the watch
(d) Someone else stole the watch
(e) You borrowed the watch
(f) You stole a cheaper watch
(g) You stole something else.

Body language

Contrary to popular belief, our word choice and delivery, as we saw earlier in this chapter, is only a small part in the effectiveness of our message. Our body language is comparatively more important. Body language is an idiom we all speak, but few actually understand. It's an extremely complex form of expression.

Body language guidelines

- Body language is subconscious. We don't necessarily understand the messages we are sending. In fact, our gestures are to a large extent unconscious. How many times has someone said to you after an interaction. You obviously did not like that person!'? Our body language will often give away our true feelings, despite what we say. If we don't like someone, it will show.

- Body language is used to communicate attitude. How you feel on a certain day will show in your body language and in your voice. It's how you show interest.

- Body language is culturally influenced. It varies from culture to culture and what is acceptable in one culture may not be in another. Without realising this difference, we can make incorrect judgements about customers and their messages, or accidentally offend them by our own gestures. For instance, in some cultures not making eye contact is a sign of respect. In western culture, not making direct eye contact can be viewed as a lack of confidence or interest.

- Body language is also used to communicate power. Standing up when someone else is sitting or infringing another's space are both examples of how body language is used to exert dominance. As service providers, we must be careful not to make customers feel we are trying to exert power over them.

- When we are in harmony with customers, we subconsciously 'pace' or 'mirror' their body language. We speak at the same speed, lean towards them, nod as they nod, etc. Conversely, when we don't like a customer or are feeling defensive, we may subconsciously 'dispace' them. We may talk more slowly when they are talking quickly, we may move back, or turn away. This displacing can negatively affect the customer's experience. As service providers we can make an effort, while not appearing manipulative, to mirror the customer's pace, gestures and word choice in order to improve their perception of the customer service interaction.

- One of the most important things to remember when reading body language is that it is composed of a series of signals, not just one or two. Folding the arms combined with lifting the shoulders, putting the chin down and a severe facial expression could indicate the customer doesn't agree with what is being said. Folding the arms *only* is not necessarily a signal of disinterest: it could simply be a more comfortable position. Don't interpret only one sign since combined with other actions it could mean something else.

Body language components
Body language is made up of:

- **Eye contact and movements**. Making direct eye contact with the customer is a way to build a relationship, though too much eye contact can be seen as dominating or intimidating.

Remember that rolling the eyes will obviously not communicate a positive customer service attitude!

- **Facial expression**. Stress and emotions are often reflected in facial expressions. A smile uses more muscles than a frown, so exercise your smile!

- **Movement**. Moving around can add energy to the interaction, but too much movement in a person-to-person interaction may cause discomfort and be viewed as boredom by the customer.

- **Posture and stance**. Holding yourself upright can communicate confidence; taken to an extreme, it could denote arrogance. Don't wriggle or twitch. Don't cross your legs or lean unnecessarily. Watch barriers and move around them when you can. When a customer changes posture this is often an indication that a change in communication mode is required.

- **Space**. We each carry around our unique bubbles of space. We have three space bubbles: intimate, personal and professional. If we go into the customer's space, they will pull back and feel pressured. We can use this knowledge in two ways. First, when we want to take control of an interaction we can physically move forward. Second, when we want to make the other person feel comfortable we can step back.

- **Gestures**. There are over 30 gestures in all that can enhance the effectiveness of our message including open hands, nodding and palms up. Unacceptable gestures are pointings and beckoning.

- **Dress**. It's important to dress appropriately for the business situation. When we first meet someone our style of dress affects our credibility.

- **Breathing**. Our stress level will effect our breathing. When we are stressed our breathing becomes shallow and fast. Unconsciously, the customer can pick this up and also be affected. When you are stressed, calm your breathing; it will help you to relax and get oxygen to your brain so that you can think clearly.

- **Natural self**. We each possess a unique identity when interacting with a customer. It is important to assess our natural self to see how to improve its effectiveness, yet remain genuine. If we try to modify our style based on other people's styles, we'll come across as insincere. By all means watch other techniques but adapt them to your own natural style.

EXERCISE

Body language

The best way to get a perspective on your body language is to videotape yourself conducting a role-play with a 'pretend' customer. Watch for the body language components discussed above.

1 What were the gestures you used effectively?
2 How was your posture?
3 How long did you make eye contact with the customer? Were any eye movements distracting?
4 How well did you mirror or pace the customer?
5 What movement were you making? To what extent did it help/hinder the interaction?
6 How would you describe your natural self with the customer?

Body language on the phone
Often individuals have to interact with customers on the phone. Even on the phone most people can hear a smile in the voice, either through the tone or the energy exuded. So even if customers can't see you, chances are they know when you are paying attention and are motivated, and when you are distracted and not interested. The statistics we quoted earlier are different if you are on the phone: 14 per cent of the message comes from the words themselves, 86 per cent is from the delivery. One of the oldest recommendations for those giving customer service on the phone is to 'stand up and smile' as you answer the phone.

COMMUNICATING THREE DIFFERENT WAYS

There are three styles of communication:

- aggressive
- submissive
- assertive.

Aggressive communication

Communication becomes aggressive when we stand up for our own rights in such a way that the other person's rights are violated. It's when we express thoughts, feelings and beliefs in unsuitable and inappropriate ways, even if we may honestly view our beliefs to be right. Aggression gives us the advantage at the expense of others and often serves to degrade others. It leads to a closedown in communication.

Submissive communication

When we use submissive communication we fail to stand up for our rights or we express them in a way that allows others to easily disregard them. We are submissive when we express our thoughts, values and beliefs in an apologetic, cautious or self-effacing manner, or do not express our ideas at all. We also might use long, justifying explanations, often putting ourselves down while submitting to the wants and needs of others. It leads to win-lose communication, where neither party is satisfied.

Assertive communication

Both aggressive and submissive communication are 'automatic'. They originate from the body's fight (aggressive) or flight (submissive) response. Assertive communication is the most misunderstood: it involves standing up for our own rights, in a way that does not violate another person's. It requires a conscious and deliberate choice as it supersedes our body's natural reactions. It leads to an open and honest communication of our own point of view while at the same time showing we understand the other person's position.

For instance, if asked by a customer for something that's completely unrealistic (a fairly common occurrence!) the replies could be:

- Aggressive: You have got to be kidding – that's completely unrealistic!

- Submissive: Well I guess we could do that, er . . .

- Assertive: I understand you have some critical requirements. Let's discuss what we can do to meet your needs.

EXERCISE

Aggressive, submissive and assertive communication

Write down the details of a situation when you have received an unrealistic request from a colleague or customer.

List an aggressive, submissive and assertive response.

CHECKLIST

1 Did you list words that might inhibit communication effectiveness?
2 Did you complete the exercise on delivery?
3 Did you tape yourself to observe your body language?
4 Did you try out aggressive, submissive and assertive communication?

CASE STUDIES

Kitchen Barn trains its people

Kitchen Barn used their internal training department as a partner in developing and rolling out customer service training. Gary decided to initiate wall-to-wall training: every person in every store would be trained, no matter how long they had worked for the company. The purpose of this approach was to ensure that all people heard the same message at the same time.

The training department had only two people so it was decided to train the district managers to run the programme. Facilitation skills and coaching skills are remarkably similar and Gary thought that if they couldn't facilitate, maybe they shouldn't be managers.

The following approach was used to institutionalise the customer service training.

1 The training director, with the help of store personnel, developed a training programme based on her assessment of the competencies and skills required.
2 The programme coined the acronym GUEST for its customer service philosophy:

G: Greet the customer
U: Understand customer needs
E: Explain features and benefits
S: Suggest additional items
T: Thank the customer.

3 With the successful completion of this programme the training director then created a leader's guide and visual aids so that any trainer could run it.
4 She then conducted a train-the-trainer programme for all district managers.
5 The trainers ran the programme for each of their stores (most district managers had approximately 11 stores).

This approach meant that every store person could be trained in a six-week time period (over 4,500 sales associates). The programme was extremely successful and as a result it was rolled out on a once-a-year basis.

The advantages of this 'roll-down' approach are:

• Many people can be trained in a short time.

• The management team owns responsibility for the training.

• The management team is then able to provide follow-up coaching and reinforcement.

The possible disadvantages of this approach are:

• Consistent quality of all the training is difficult to ensure.

• The district managers could find it hard to take the time to prepare to run the programme.

• Fluency in the programme could be lost if training does not occur often enough.

• The entire management team was removed from its 'real job' for six weeks.

Internet Express trains its people

Internet Express decided to bring in consultants to train its Field Engineers and help desk staff. They believed that the 'outside expert' perspective was required for technical employees to really understand the importance of these interpersonal 'soft' skills. The programme was customised to the company's needs in the following way:

- The consultants sat in the call centre and visited customer sites with the field engineers.

- Based on the data collected they customised the programme to this specific market segment in the following way:
  —All exercises were geared to the company.
  —The role plays were based around TARs (technical assistance requests) that the consultant had observed.

The agenda for the programme was as shown below.

Managing Customer Perceptions	
Introduction	• facilitator welcome • ice-breaker/introductions • objectives/agenda • role of technical support
The business environment and customer service	• customer service quiz • the importance of customer service • material and personal service • internal and external customers • moments of truth
Maximising communication	• communication exercise • understanding communication • components of communication • sending the message, communicating with the customer – role plays
Managing the customer interaction	• step one: start the interaction • step two: establish the customer's agenda • step three: establish a plan • step four: finish the interaction • video tape 'real world' role-plays —setting customer expectations

	—no 'transparency' —dealing assertively with customer requests —communicating effectively while doing damage control —handling customer conflicts
Dealing with difficult customer situations	• utilise the CLEAR technique —calm your emotions —listen actively: content and exercise —empathise with the customer: content and exercise —apologise to the customer: content and exercise —resolve the situation: content and exercise • how to respond when the process does not meet the customer's needs • video-taped role plays • feedback

ACTION POINTS

1 How much emphasis have you placed on training your service providers with interpersonal skills? What training classes have they been sent to? How else could you improve their personal communication skills?

2 To what extent do you hear your people using assertive communication? How could you support them in using assertive rather than aggressive or submissive styles?

6

Managing the Customer Interaction

In the last chapter we described the personal service skills involved in sending an effective message. As we stated, communication is the exchange of information between the sender and the receiver. In this chapter we focus on the communication skills required to successfully manage the customer interaction and obtain a response from the customer. By setting customer expectations appropriately, we stand a better chance of being able to exceed these expectations and keep the customer coming back. Moments of truth happen when all the service skills introduced combine to create a customer impression, either positive or negative. We will revisit moments of truth in some detail, and provide examples of specific ones that the companies in our case studies faced and addressed successfully.

THE CUSTOMER INTERACTION MODEL

The customer interaction model to produce the BEST result has four steps:

B: **B**egin the customer interaction
      —gauge mood
      —build rapport

E: **E**stablish the customer's agenda
      —ask open-ended and closed questions
      —be quiet
      —listen actively
      —probe for specifics
      —paraphrase

S: **S**atisfy the customer's needs
      —generate more than one option
      —consider the customer's perspective

T: Thank the customer and verify the next step
    —thank the customer
    —verify who will do what by when.

Step one: begin the customer interaction

> First impressions are lasting ones.

What makes a lasting impression on customers is the way they are treated at the beginning of an interaction. Interestingly it can take only 30 seconds to get a first impression: the body language shows disinterest, the tone of voice is lethargic, etc. We need to make sure the initial interaction is a positive, impressive one.

In this step we want to:

- Gauge the customer's mood by observing their body language in terms of facial expressions, pace, movement, etc. As you assess the customer, it is important to not pre-judge – all customers are created equal and appearances can be deceptive.

- Establish professional rapport with the customer by mirroring their pace, energy and word choice. For instance, if the customer is in a hurry and is speaking quickly, you need to get to the point quickly. If the customer is moving more slowly and engages us in conversation, it could appear rude if you try to move on to establishing the customer's agenda before they are ready.

- Rapport can also be established by conducting small-talk on either personal or professional issues. For instance you could discuss the general business situation within the company.

- You'll know when to move on to the next step of the interaction when the customer changes posture in some way: by picking up a pencil, leaning forward, etc. It's then time to move to the most important step in managing the interaction: establishing the customer's agenda.

Step two: establish the customer's agenda

Don't assume

The purpose of this step is to understand what the customer wants and/or needs. You will need to use some essential communication skills to gather the most complete information possible before jumping in to meet the customer's needs, or to resolve a situation.

Ask open-ended questions
There are two types of questions: open-ended and closed. Open-ended questions cannot be answered by a yes or no and serve to open up communication. They are designed to gather information and data about the customer's requirements.

In our society we are not very good at asking open-ended questions since we don't want to waste time. Open-ended questions may appear to be more time-consuming initially but save time in the long run since they result in a more positive and productive interaction.

Open-ended questions begin with the words: tell me about, describe, explain, who, what, where, when, why and how. Examples are:

- Tell me about the approach that you wish to take.
- Explain what you have done previously.
- Describe the critical steps in this process.
- What is your idea?
- How can we improve the existing set-up?

EXERCISE

Open-ended questions
Change the following questions to open-ended questions.

1 Have you checked the hardware in the system?
2 Do you have any questions?
3 Have you any other needs?

Answers

1   What changes have you made to the hardware in the system?
     When was the last time you checked the system hardware?
2   What questions can I answer for you?
     What other issues do you need help with?
3   What other services can I offer you today?
     What other needs do you have in terms of system per-
     formance?

Closed questions

Closed questions can be answered by a yes or no and serve to
gather specific data. They normally begin with an auxiliary verb
such as can, will, have and did. They are used to close down a part
of the conversation and to verify actual information. Examples of
closed questions are:

- Do you have any questions?

- Is that all?

- Do you want three or four?

Either type of question is good as long as it serves to gather
relevant information or helps move the interaction in a positive
way.

Wait for the response

Too often when we ask open-ended questions, we are either too
impatient or too uncomfortable with the silence to wait for an
answer. We then either answer our own question, or ask another
one or the same question again. As a result the customer may get
confused and become reluctant to give us the information we
need. Remember that silence is golden. If you answer your own
question it will set the tone that you don't expect an answer. Make
sure you allow time for a response: this can take between two to
ten seconds.

Active listening

Listening is an art. Once developed, it can be priceless.

Good listening is one of the most complex communication skills yet one that receives poor attention in our society.

- At school we spent over ten years being taught how to speak, while no instruction was given on how to listen. Being seen and not heard is not the same as learning how to listen.

- Our society often places power with the speaker not the listener, so we tend to view listening as a passive activity.

- Our brains can process information at over 250 words per minute, yet we can only speak at about 125 words per minute. As a result, half the time we are listening we are bored.

- Common barriers to listening include rehearsing (practising what you are going to say while the other person is talking), boredom, lack of interest and stereotyping.

- In reality, listening is an active skill that gives control of the conversation to the service provider who is listening. Good listening is a prerequisite to good customer service.

Improving your listening skills
Below are a few ideas to help you improve your listening skills.

1 Pay attention to the other person. Stop your mind from wandering as they are speaking. Many people write notes while the customer speaks (in sales/telephone interactions) to help focus on the customer's words. If you take notes, write only key words. Writing the customer's words verbatim won't help your listening skills!
2 Process the information as the customer is speaking. Try to view the data from their perspective.
3 Be patient if their communication style or pacing is different from yours.
4 Don't dismiss or judge the speaker because of their appearance. Listen to what they have to say.
5 If you find yourself rehearsing, ask questions to gather more data.
6 Probe for specifics. Probing for specifics is the skill of taking the basic information received, repeating it, and asking further open-ended questions to gather more specific data within the subject area.

Paraphrasing

Paraphrasing is a listening skill that can be used to clarify the meaning of a customer's statement. It is rephrasing in your own words what the customer has said. Paraphrasing is particularly useful if the customer has given you a lot of complex information. It has two main benefits:

1 Paraphrasing lets the customer know you have digested the information that has been shared and allows you to correct any possible errors in your understanding.
2 Paraphrasing validates the customer's perspective by showing that you heard what was said. This can build the customer's trust and respect.

Paraphrasing is:

- *not* parroting back word for word what the customer has just said.

- Capturing the content of the customer's message in an abbreviated format.

- *not* making judgements or providing your own perspective.

- Showing that you have understood the feelings, as well as the content of the message being expressed.

- Distilling the essence of the customer's words, paying attention to the underlying meaning.

EXERCISE

Listening

1 Listen to the news on the radio.
2 Make notes of the key points.
3 Repeat the highlights back to a friend or another person, and let them give you feedback on how effectively you listened.

Step three: satisfy the customer's needs

People don't buy products. They buy solutions.

- It is always necessary to generate more than one alternative so you have a fallback plan if the first option fails. Try to generate as many solutions as possible before you go into the evaluation mode. By jumping to a solution too quickly, you may eliminate a better solution.

- Too often we react to the first problem or need without considering more long-term or proactive approaches. This approach can limit our effectiveness in exceeding customers' expectations. We must consider both reactive and proactive approaches to satisfying customers' needs.

- We tend to think about the best approach from our own perspective. We need to think about ideas and possibilities also from the customer's perspective.

- We have to be sure to satisfy the real customer need. Often when the second stage of the interaction is neglected, we miss the important moments of truth in the interaction (see the examples later in the chapter) which results in not meeting the customer's real need.

Step four: thank the customer and verify the next steps

> Thanking the customer is not the end. It's a new beginning.

At the end of the interaction we need to:

- Ensure the customer is satisfied. This is normally achieved by asking!

- Confirm/verify the above (remember what, who, when) by summarising the key data at the end of the interaction. Taking time in this area can ensure we start the next interaction in a positive way. Too often, the customer and the service provider leave the interaction with vastly different expectations.

MOMENTS OF TRUTH

As we discussed in Chapter 2, moments of truth are the specific milestones in the customer interaction when the customer's judgement of the service interaction is made. They are similar to crossroads where you can take a wrong turn and create problems that you'll need to recover from later, or where you make the right decision and build a positive customer impression. By combining multiple postive moments of truth, we create happy customers; multiple negative moments of truth can create unhappy customers.

As we discussed earlier not all moments of truth are created equally. Some carry greater weight than others. Using the service skills described in this and the previous chapter will help to ensure that you recognise and respond appropriately to every moment of truth.

Some moments of truth are related to material service (process/ product issues/queue, etc), some are related to internal service (someone else not being able to rewrite the software), and some are related to your listening to and understanding the cutomer issues.

> No matter what the source of the moments of truth, you, as the service provider, have to use professional communication skills to move on in a positive way in the interaction and meet the customer's expectations.

In any one interaction there could be as many as 40 moments of truth; while we are managing one, we may miss the others and disappoint our customers.

For instance in a 'routine' technical support call the following moments of truth arose:

- Long queue time.
- New person in the position, therefore incomplete product knowledge.
- The product had repeatedly failed.
- The 'patch' that was supposed to fix the problem didn't.
- The person who had been dealing with the issue had failed to get back to the customer within the promised time frame.
- The organisation recently merged with another, and many of the development engineers had left.

- The call tracking system was out of date and overloaded.

- The sales person had oversold the product and its capabilities.

Any one of these issues alone could create a dissatisfied customer, but the combination created multitudes of precarious moments of truth. The customer service representative felt as if he were trying to manoeuvre through a minefield!

Using moments of truth positively
When trying to optimise customer service it is important to:

1 Identify the most common moments of truth for the customer, based on your current business situation.
2 Help those providing customer service to script professional answers so they can appropriately address these issues.

Examples

- Long queue time.
  —don't ignore!
  —don't say 'I know – I've told management but they haven't done anything about it yet'
  —apologise
  —say 'the current version of the product is proving very popular'
  —say 'this time of day often has a higher call volume'
  —say 'management is aware of the issue and is working on it'.

Then use a transition phrase to move onto the real reason the customer called; 'Let's move on to resolve the technical issues.'

- You don't know the information.
  —don't bluff – body language will give you away
  —don't say 'I don't know'
  —say 'I don't know, however I can find out'
  —find the right resources.

EXERCISE

Moments of truth
Think about some moments of truth for your service:

1 What changes have you made to systems recently?
2 What organisational changes have taken place that might impact the customer?
3 What product/service issues do you know about?
4 What complaints have you received recently?

List these moments of truth and then pick *one*:

1 What do you feel you *shouldn't* say about this moment of truth?
2 How could you describe this situation positively to the customer?
3 What else could you do to ensure this moment of truth has a positive outcome?

CHECKLIST

1 Did you complete the exercise changing closed questions to open-ended questions?
2 Did you try listening to the news and paraphrasing your ideas back to a friend?
3 Did you identify the important moments of truth that your business is experiencing right now?

CASE STUDIES

Kitchen Barn manages its moments of truth

Kitchen Barn had created scripts/ideas for some of the most thorny moments of truth such as:

— Why are you more expensive than Asda?
— Some of these products look too fragile.

● *Why are you more expensive than Asda?* Sometimes it appears that our products are more expensive than the larger superstores. However, for the most part we have found that we offer a higher quality product, with a greater range of features supported by the service we provide. Often our products therefore prove to be more reliable and resilient.

- *Some of these products look too fragile.* We specialise in a specific aesthetic look. At the same time our buyers ensure the best quality design and materials used. So even if they look fragile they have proved to be quality products.

Internet Express manages its moments of truth

Internet Express used consultants to identify the difficult moments of truth that the team in the support centre were facing. Some of the specific moments of truth the group needed help scripting were:

- *Company merged.* The company had recently merged with another company, both companies had changed their names, and the cultures and service approaches of the two were very different. In addition, many of the company's original employees had decided to leave because they were uncomfortable with the new management philosophy. Often customers said things such as 'When you were . . . Inc, you were much more customer focused,' 'I heard that most of your engineers have left.' Some of the ideas to address these comments were:

  —'We have experienced some growing pains in the transition.'
  —'We are in the process of rebuilding and integrating the two technical support functions.'
  —'There has been some turnover of staff which is very common in such a dynamic industry/organisation.'
  —'We are currently integrating all our services into one location.'
  —'I am sorry – I assure you we are diligently working to improve customer service.'

- *Existing problem.* There was a known bug in one specific product that had not been corrected initially. After some time the company created a patch for the bug, but had only proactively communicated this patch to the Gold Service customers. Often customers said things such as 'If you already knew about the problem, why didn't you let me know about it?' Some of the ideas to address these comments were:

  —'We have just received a patch that resolves this issue.'

—'We have been testing to ensure that the patch really does resolve this specific issue.'

- *Sales person oversold the product and has now been fired.* Often sales people describe the product or service in over-generous terms in their enthusiasm to close a deal. In addition, based on the need to make a quota, turnover on the sales team is normally quite high. The company obviously does not want the service engineer to say 'You know sales people they'll do anything to get a commission!' Some of the ideas to address these comments were:

  —'Often the sales person has recommended a product/service based on your current business environment. As your business grows, the original specifications may not be adequate to meet your needs.'
  —'It may be that your business load has changed and the requirements for your system are now different. Let's look at how we could assess your current needs.'
  —'Sales people do move around frequently as the market changes – he is no longer here. However I can find the name of the new sales person or the sales manager for you.'

The training programmes provided a valuable forum for the group to discuss appropriate answers to these sticky questions. The result was that each engineer created a 'toolbox' of possible words and phrases to use to manage those difficult moments of truth effectively. Some of these ideas were transcribed and included in a FAQ (frequently asked questions) manual so they had easier access to the data in those stressful moments.

ACTION POINTS

1   How can you help service providers use the BEST technique to manage the moments of truth effectively?

2   B: How can you ensure service providers are positive when they greet the customer at the beginning of the inter-action?

3   E: How can you create standard or suggested open-ended

questions to ask in ascertaining customer needs first? How can you ensure they paraphrase the customer's response?

4 S: How can you reinforce suggesting more than one solution in meeting customer needs?

5 T: How can you ensure they finish the interaction with a clear understanding of who has to do what by when?

6 To what extent have you identified the moments of truth that service providers in your business face on a regular basis and scripted responses to help them deal with these issues? How could you begin or fine-tune this process?

7

Establishing Effective Processes

As we discussed in earlier chapters, service providers use personal skills to capitalise on moments of truth and exceed customer expectations. However, effective processes and procedures provide the foundation for smoothing or inhibiting the customer interaction. Efficient service delivery systems appear transparent to the customer. Poor systems create those 'speed bumps' that necessitate personal intervention in order to satisfy the customer requirements. In this chapter we describe how to establish effective service standards and objectives, and then evaluate the performance of our service delivery processes against these standards. Finally we review how our profiled companies approached defining their service standards and measuring the effectiveness of their systems.

CREATING SERVICE OBJECTIVES AND STANDARDS

One of the most important facets in managing service excellence is to define specific service standards and objectives, and then measure and adjust performance to exceed these principles.

> It is a sure fact, if you don't know where you are going there is a good chance that you will end up somewhere else!

There are two main criteria we use to create our target of effective service: **objectives** and **standards**.

- Objectives are concrete, measurable outcomes from specific projects.

- Standards define the minimal acceptable performance level within a specific category.

Let's review each in a little more detail.

Establishing service objectives

Objectives are concrete, tangible, measurable results or outcomes that result from our efforts; they are the deliverables we produce. They tend to be more project-focused. Effective objectives need to be SMART:

S: Specific. Does it home in on a particular performance component?

M: Measurable. What are the quantity, quality specifications, cost and revenue, etc?

A: Aligned. Is it aligned with the organisation's vision/mission and the customer service strategy?

R: Results-focused. Does it lead to a tangible result?

T: Time-based. Does it have a specific due date?

Example

• Incorrect: to contact five prospects by 31 January 20XX.

This is a task, and it does not tell us what the result is, or why we are doing it.

• Correct: to obtain one client with revenue or £XXXXX by contacting five prospects for training services, by 31 January 20XX.

You can see that this is an effective objective because it is:

Specific:	one client
Measurable:	size of revenue
Aligned:	with the vision
Results-focused:	the outcome, not what you will do to get there
Time-based:	by 31 January 20XX.

Differentiating between objectives and tasks

In order to differentiate between objectives and tasks, ask three questions:

• What's the result?

- What's the benefit of taking this approach?

- Why are we doing this?

Writing down objectives

Too often we write tasks and not objectives, because tasks are the things that we *do*. However, if there is no benefit, or result, or reason why we are doing it, it is a task and maybe one of those tasks we should not be doing at all.

It is important to define and write down objectives for as many aspects of service delivery as we can. Research conducted on Yale students 20 years after they had graduated showed that 3 per cent were earning more money than the other 97 per cent combined. The only difference was that the 3 per cent had *written down their objectives* after graduation.

> There is something about writing down objectives that affirms our commitment to them, and keeps them in sight and in mind.

Sometimes it is hard to be specific when writing subjective objectives. For instance, when considering improving communication it's hard to quantify this increase. In this case, standards can be used as the measurement device, eg number of meetings, speed in returning calls, customer feedback, etc.

Make sure you use words in your objective statements such as ensure, increase, reduce, obtain, achieve, attain, raise, etc.

Examples of sample customer service objectives

1 To raise customer satisfaction levels, as measured by the XYZ survey, from 5.9 to 6.5 by 1 January 20XX.
2 To obtain feedback from 20% of our registered customer base, on our current range of services by 1 July 20XX.

Tasks to create objectives

The tasks we have to complete, with the specific milestones (the deadlines) can then be mapped out to achieve these service objectives. Tasks and milestones for a sample service objective, that are within the **key result area** (KRA) customer service, are shown below:

KRA	Objective(s)
Customer service	To obtain feedback from 20% of our registered customer base on our current range of services by 1 July 20XX

Tasks and activities necessary to complete the objective

Number	What?	Who?	When	Completed
1	Update database	JK	31 January 20XX	
2	Decide 20% of users who will be targeted	BA	28 February 20XX	
3	Design flyer/ questionnaire	CL	14 March 20XX	
4	Distribute questionnaire	BA	31 March 20XX	
5	Collate results	CL	31 March – 14 June	
6	Summarise results	CL	30 June 20XX	

EXERCISE

Creating a customer service objective with associated tasks and milestones

1 Draw up a table like the one above and write one of your customer service objectives.

2 Make sure it is SMART.
   —**S**pecific
   —**M**easurable

　　　—**A**ligned
　　　—**R**esults-focused
　　　—**T**ime-based.

3　Ask yourself the following questions to ensure you are writing
　objectives and not tasks:
　　　—What's the result?
　　　—What's the benefit?
　　　—Why are we doing this?
4　Then complete the tasks and milestones (dates) to achieve this.

KRA	Objective(s)
Customer service	

Tasks and activities necessary to complete the objective				
Number	**What?**	**Who?**	**When**	**Completed**
1				
2				
3				
4				
5				
6				

DEFINING SERVICE STANDARDS

As we discussed earlier, for workload that is continuous it can
be difficult to write objectives that are specific and measurable
with a specific delivery date. Areas that tend to be ongoing are
communication, administration, etc. Also many of the personal
service skills we discussed in Chapters 5 and 6, and the skills for

resolving irate customer situations to be introduced in Chapter 8, require standards versus concrete objectives too.

Examples of standards in relation to customer service as a framework for performance could be:

- Reply to all phone calls within 24 hours.
- Reply to all e-mails within 48 hours.
- Queue times no more than 20 minutes.
- Always apologise at least once to irate customers.
- Use at least five open-ended questions in identifying needs.
- Paraphrase back key data at least once per conversation.

The purpose of these standards is to establish a minimal acceptance performance level. Often when multiple standards are combined, they will result in an objective being achieved. For instance, if you reduce the queue time and fix all level one problems within 24 hours you would be well on the way to scoring highly on a customer satisfaction survey. (Always assuming you have used the correct personal service skills with the customer!)

TRACKING THE CUSTOMER CYCLE

The next step in creating customer standards for your organisation is to track the steps in the customer experience. By doing this, you can identify the standards and the processes required to smooth the interaction at these points. We briefly discussed the steps in the customer service cycle in Chapter 2 in 'Assessing your current customer service'.

For instance the service cycle at a hotel might include the following steps:

- Customer gathers data on the hotel from research on the web, a brochure or a travel agent.
- Customer may try to book via the web or via a telephone.
- Customer books and receives a confirmation.
- Customer calls for directions.
- Customer arrives outside the hotel.

- Customer checks in.
- Customer goes to the room.
- Customer tries to make a phone call/use e-mail.
- Customer calls room service.
- Customer organises and receives a wake-up call.
- Customer uses hotel bar/restaurant.
- Customer uses work-out facilities.
- Customer, during their stay, enters and leaves the hotel.
- Housekeeping cleans the room.
- Customer uses room facilities: bathroom, TV, etc.
- Customer checks out.
- Customer leaves hotel.

As you can see, there are numerous opportunities to make or break the service experience! Identifying these steps, in detail, and then determining standards for them will result in a more consistent meeting of customer expectations.

Examples of standards could be:

- Customer uses work-out facilities:
  —clean towels constantly available
  —all equipment working
  —drinking water provided.

- Customer enters and leaves hotel:
  —doorman to greet every customer with a smile
  —staff to remember names of customers who stay more than three days
  —entrance lobby clean and free from litter.

EXERCISE

Creating a set of customer service standards for your area

1 Draw up a table like the one below and recreate the steps in your customer service cycle.

2 Brainstorm, for each step, some customer service standards for areas that are ongoing and/or related to personal service delivery.
3 Make sure they have a specific frequency associated with them.

Step in the customer service cycle	Service standards	Frequency

ASSESSING SYSTEMS REQUIRED

Once we have identified the steps in the cycle and the standards for each, it is important to assess what systems and procedures can facilitate service delivery to achieve these standards. For instance the following service processes have been instituted in the New York Palace Hotel to produce consistent results.

When bellboys show new customers to their rooms, they conduct a guided tour of the bedroom showing all 'gadgets' (and there are quite a few), and describe the services of the hotel.

Instead of the do not disturb sign (that inevitably gets lost or moved), there are electronic do not disturb signs centrally controlled from the side of the bed.

If housekeepers are unable to perform the nightly turn-down service because the do not disturb light is on, they will call the room and offer to return later.

EXERCISE

Evaluating your customer service delivery systems

1 Draw up a table like the one below and recreate the steps in your customer service cycle.
2 List the standards alongside each.
3 Now evaluate the current systems you use to deliver these standards: how effective are they in meeting customer needs?

4   Consider if there are any systems that could be added to facilitate meeting customer needs more smoothly.
5   What systems exist that may be inhibiting service delivery: unnecessary steps in processes, redundant procedures, etc?
6   What changes will you make to your service delivery systems to exceed customer expectations?

Step in the customer service cycle	Service standards	Frequency

CHECKLIST

1   Did you write a sample service objective for your business?
2   Did you list the tasks and activities necessary to achieve the objective?
3   Did you map out specific service standards for each step in the service delivery cycle?
4   Did you evaluate the processes and systems to help you achieve these standards?

CASE STUDIES

Kitchen Barn implements effective processes

Kitchen Barn already had specific standards for both its material and personal service delivery. The standards for personal service delivery were based on the content of the GUEST approach (described in Chaper 5) and included such things as:

- Every customer to be greeted within ten seconds of entering the store.

- Every customer to be asked at least five open-ended questions.

- Every customer to be offered an additional related or non-related item.

Kitchen Barn discovered, when it analysed its current business performance that, although it was gaining new customers in different markets, there was attrition from its current customer base. As we know, it costs a lot more to get business from new customers than it does to generate more business from existing customers. Gary decided he wanted to institute a new service objective which was: 'To increase sales to existing customers by 10 per cent by 1 January 20XX, from £ . . . thousand to £ . . . thousand.'

To achieve this objective he instituted a clientele programme, to encourage existing customers to return. Components of this included:

- Each Sales Associate had a clientele book.

- Each Sales Associate, in every store, had to add three new names a week to this clientele book. To this end, specific scripts were created to be used at checkout to ask new customers for their permission to be included in this book.

- Customers entered in this clientele book were also centrally recorded on a database, and received flyers once a quarter describing new offerings.

- Stores held special 'evenings' for clientele customers, either before sales or to show new merchandise.

As a result of this effort sales to existing customers actually increased by 20 per cent, while new customers also continued to grow. A success all round, aided by a clear objective and specific standards.

Internet Express implements effective processes

Setting objectives
The following represent three objectives from the Internet Express Support Centre:

1 Raise customer satisfaction levels with frontline support from the current level of 65 per cent to 85 per cent as measured by

the monthly after-service surveys, by developing and implementing a set of problem-handling and escalation procedures, by 1 April 20XX.

2 Ensure the average speed of answer (ASA) is under three minutes for each product queue, as measured by the weekly automatic call distributor (ACD) reports, by establishing and implementing a call queue monitoring, measurement, improvement and reward process, by 20 September 20XX.

3 Raise the first-call resolution rate from the current level of 60 per cent to 80 per cent as measured by the Service Call Manager (SCM is a brand of call and problem-tracking system) monthly performance reports, by re-engineering and improving the current problem handling process, by 30 September 20XX.

The individual managers then met with their respective teams to further define individual SMART objectives with specific tasks and milestones to achieve them.

Defining service standards

The senior management team reviewed existing customer satisfaction surveys and talked with their customers regarding the specific support centre performance standards. From this work they developed a complete set of standards to cover the key areas of the Support Centre.

These standards centred on three key areas:

- Service delivery including responsiveness to service calls and problem resolution.

- Service culture.

- People motivation and skills.

The management team then worked with their Supervisors, Product Leads and Analysts to develop the performance standards. Some examples of these are shown on page 116.

Service culture performance standards

The management team worked very closely with the technical phone analysts to develop these service standards in four main areas.

Service delivery performance standards			
Performance standard	**Source**	**Standard**	**Measurement**
Average speed of answer	ACD	Less than 3 minutes average	ACD reports
Calls abandoned	ACD	Less than 5%	ACD reports
Longest wait time in queue	ACD	5 minutes	ACD reports
% of first call resolution	SCM	80%	# Closed TARs with one attached call activity/total closed TARs
% problems resolved by second-level support	SCM	15%	# TARs closed/total TARs received
Backline unresolved problem queue	SCM	Monthly rolling average less than 30	SCM problem resolution reports

- Call handling: the teams developed a structured call handling and call feedback process to cover the beginning of the call, resolution of the call and ending the call. The calls were then randomly audited each week and a feedback summary provided. As described in Chapter 7 it included standards such as:
  —asking at least three open-ended questions
  —summarising the data at the end of the call
  —paraphrasing at regular intervals, etc.

- Phone time: provide efficient service to customers as measured by an average weekly phone time of more than 30 hours.

- Dependability: adhere responsibly to the schedule as measured by on-time arrival and readiness to take calls, timely return from lunch and breaks and adequate notice of absence.

- Continuous improvement: capture all relevant data by logging 100 per cent of all calls into SCM and linking 75 per cent of the calls into the Knowledge base. Additionally add a minimum of two known solutions to the Knowledge base per week.

People motivation and skills
In this area each analyst completed the skills matrix and then developed their individual training plans in consultation with their Supervisor and Manager. The analysts were then measured on the number of classes completed and the skills matrix updated.

Senior analysts and analysts with specialised skills then gave technical talks on various areas of interest to the team and the usefulness of the talk was ranked by the team members.

ACTION POINTS

1 What service objectives will you define for your organisation/ team/group? What specific areas would produce improvements in customer satisfaction levels? How can you ensure that the objectives are specific, measurable, aligned, results-focused and time-based?

2 What specific tasks or activities need to take place in order to make these objectives a reality? How will you prioritise between multiple objectives and tasks?

3 In what areas of your business, due to the ongoing nature of the activity, do you require service standards? How can you ensure that these service standards are accurate and meet customer needs? What performance objectives do these standards help to meet?

4 Map your service cycle and create standards for each step. What steps are hard to measure? Which steps are critical for customer satisfaction to attain? How will you raise standards?

5 What additional service processes or systems would help to achieve these standards? Which service processes appear to be hindering or slowing down service to the external customer? What can you do to manage your service delivery processes on an ongoing basis?

8

Dealing with Customer Complaints

As we discussed in Chapter 2, instituting continuous improvement is the fourth leg of the service delivery model. For this subject we will break down this process into short-term recovery, to be covered in this chapter, and then examine long-term process improvements in Chapter 9.

We begin by discussing how we can ensure that our customers have ways to communicate their issues to us. We then describe recovery and its importance as a service management tool. Then we look at how we manage short-term recovery by successfully defusing angry customers using the CLEAR technique. Using this technique, we can succeed in calming our customers and obtaining relevant data for improving both personal and material service processes.

SEEKING CUSTOMER COMPLAINTS

The starting point for many of the continuous improvement initiatives can come from listening and responding to customer complaints. It is therefore necessary to ensure we provide systems to solicit regular feedback from our customers, and that we make it easy for them to complain to us. Ideas that can be implemented are:

- Suggestion boxes.
- Feedback forms.
- Providing a customer service hotline.
- Personal interaction: either face-to-face or via the telephone.
- Publicising names of management who are available.

Examples of these systems in action are:

- 'How are we doing?' forms at a restaurant provided with the bill.

- Special phone numbers in hotels for customer service issues.

- Telephone calls after a car service to ascertain the customer's satisfaction with the service provided.

For your business, think about how you currently manage complaints, and think about one additional action you could take to encourage your customers to tell you what is not working for them. This will also help you get positive feedback on what *is* working so you know what elements of your service provide the customer with the greatest value.

DEFINING RECOVERY

Recovery is defined in the book *Service America* (see Further Reading) as 'the ability of front-line/customer-contact people to make things right for the customer when they have somehow gone astray.'

Too often, service providers regard customer complaints as a nuisance, take them personally, or deny all knowledge ('it's not my fault, it's the process'). In fact, every time a customer complains they are really telling you that they want to continue to do business with you. As you remember from the customer service quiz in Chapter 1, customers who don't care simply take their business and walk away. They don't tell *you*, but they do tell lots of other people on the way! Customers who do complain can prove to be more loyal customers, if their complaints are handled in a satisfactory way.

Unfortunately, many opportunities are missed because the moments of truth with irate customers are not managed effectively, resulting in the possible defection of a customer to another company, and the definite loss of relevant business data. In order to recover successfully, we will introduce you to the CLEAR technique that can help you manage these thorny interactions with irate customers.

USING THE CLEAR TECHNIQUE

Understanding and practising the skills in the CLEAR technique will help you to work through even the most challenging situations. Again we have used an acronym as a tool for retention. However, remember that the steps do not always happen in sequence – life would be much easier if they did, but people are rarely logical in this process.

The steps in the CLEAR technique are:

C: **C**alm your emotions
L: **L**isten actively to the customer
E: **E**mpathise with the customer
A: **A**pologise/**A**cknowledge the customer situation
R: provide reactive and proactive **R**esolution.

In most situations there is a temptation to jump straight to the resolution stage. After all, the customer is upset with the situation and if you fix it, they'll be happy – right? Wrong! Even if the problem is resolved, the customer might feel unacknowledged or unsupported in the process.

Let me tell you a story to illustrate the point. My husband and I were born in the UK, but have lived in the United States for 12 years. For our first Christmas, as we had no other extended family with us in the USA, we decided to go out for Christmas Day dinner, just the four of us: my husband, our two children and I.

The following are the key points:

- When we arrived at the restaurant the place looked like a zoo – people dashing around, with no apparent structure to the activity.

- We ordered our dinner – it arrived an hour later and it was cold.

- When we asked for a hot meal, the server took away the plates. She returned a little while later with plates that had obviously been zapped in the microwave: the outside was steaming hot, the inside lukewarm and there was this delightful congealed rim on the outside of the plate!

- We asked to talk to the manager, who, when she arrived at the table, leaned over us and said 'So, do you want a free meal?'

- Obviously we did not expect a free meal, but if she was going to offer, of course we will accept. So we had a free meal for Christmas.

- Were we then satisfied with the experience? No. Why not? Obviously we felt we had not been listened to or treated with respect. In fact the restaurant lost out two ways. Not only did they lose a customer, but they lost the money from all four dinners as well.

- We have since told *many* other people – and surprise – the restaurant chain has gone out of business. Not our work alone I'm sure, but we certainly made a contribution.

The situation could have been resolved successfully if the manager had taken the following steps:

- She needed to **calm** her emotions. Obviously she was frustrated she was working on Christmas Day; she probably had all reserve staff (who wants to work on Christmas Day after all?) and the restaurant was much busier than she expected. If she had taken some time to control her emotions, she would have been more able to assertively manage the situation.

- She then needed to **listen** actively to our description of the situation. By asking open-ended questions, listening actively and paraphrasing, she probably could have found out a little more about the importance, to us, of this Christmas dinner. Questions such as 'I hear you have had some problems with your meal, tell me a little more about them,' 'What other problems have you experienced?' etc. If the questions had been effective, I probably would have told her not only that the meals were cold, but that this was our first Christmas away from home, and that we really had wanted to make it special by eating at this restaurant.

- She then had the opportunity to **empathise** with us. While she could have demonstrated empathy by using body language, she could also have used a couple of empathy statements, such as 'I can understand you feeling frustrated because the food was cold. It sounds as if we have really contributed to upsetting your first Christmas away from your homeland.'

- She could then have **apologised** to us, not using my least favourite apology from restaurants: 'I'm sorry *but* we're busy.' Of course they are busy – that's why they are called a restaurant! Rather 'I'm sorry the food and the service has not met your expectations.'

- Then she could have asked me for my ideas for a suitable **resolution**: 'What would it take to meet your needs?' We probably would have said: 'A hot meal and a free dessert would be great'. A lot less than the amount she actually gave.

So let's look at each of these steps in some detail.

OUTLINING THE CLEAR TECHNIQUE

C: Calm your emotions

The first factor you have to address when customers are irate is managing your emotional response. As you can see from the graph in Figure 5, the more emotional you are the lower your level of logic is. Even if the resolution is the ideal, the customer won't hear it because they are still upset. Conversely, when the customer's emotions are low the logic is high, and the customer is more likely to accept the resolution.

So the first step in managing irate customers is to calm your

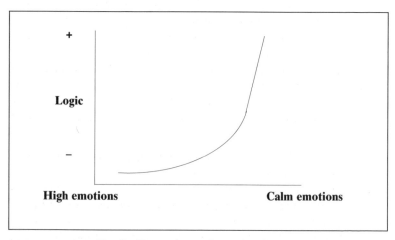

Fig. 5. Reasoning and emotions graph.

emotions, so that you can use logic and assertive communication to resolve the situation.

Some ideas that have helped calm emotions are:

- Take a deep breath (being careful not to exhale with a big sigh!).

- Mentally step back and look at the big picture.

- Realise that the customer is not directly angry at you: they are probably angry because of the situation, or because of something else going on in their life and you just happen to be on the receiving end (the traffic was bad, the cat threw up on the carpet, their boss just moaned at them, etc).

L: Listen actively to the customer

The next three steps in the CLEAR technique – the L, E, A – are geared towards calming/managing the customer's emotions. Only when the customer has also calmed down is it possible to resolve the situation.

In order to manage the customer's emotions, you have to be aware of what those emotions are. We do this by using active listening. Active listening is imperative when the customer is irate.

As you listen to the customer you need to identify:

- The content or the reason why they are feeling dissatisfied with your product or service.

- The feeling or emotion they are expressing.

Airline example

For instance, if I said 'I can't believe my suitcase is not on the same plane as I am':

- The content or the reason why I am dissatisfied is obvious: *I do not have my bag*.

- The feelings or emotions I might be experiencing are broad and could include:

 —*Worry* that I might never see the possessions in that suitcase again.
 —*Annoyance* over the hassle of getting the money back and filling in numerous forms in order to do so.

—*Frustration* because of the inconvenience.
—*Tiredness* because transatlantic flights are exhausting.

As you can see, understanding the content is the easy part. Recognising the possible range of emotions is more complex. Of course to some airlines this is a regular occurence, so to them it's no big deal: 99.9 per cent of people get their bags back – why are you upset?!' This is where the disconnection can start between the service provider and the customer.

EXERCISE

Active listening exercise
We will be using one scenario to try on the skills introduced in the L, E, A, R. The purpose of this approach is to practise each skill, separately from the others, before you put them all together. Obviously in real life all four skills could be included in one statement, as you will see.

For the customer statement, identify both the content (the reason the customer is feeling dissatisfied) and the feelings (the range of emotions) being expressed. The answers are at the end.

Customer situation: 'This is the third time you have promised delivery of these products and you have missed the dates.'

1 Describe the content (reason the customer is dissatisfied).
2 Describe the feelings (emotions being expressed).

In this situation the content, or the reason the customer is upset, is fairly easy to recognise and fix. However, if the problem is fixed without the customer feeling heard, the resolution will not be viewed as acceptable. You may have fixed the problem, but you have not fixed the customer.

Answers
1 Content: missed/unreliable shipping dates.
2 Feelings: customer feels let down, doesn't know if they can trust what you say. They may also be subject to retribution inside their company for not doing their job well enough.

E: Empathise with the customer

In active listening we identified the content or reason the customer was dissatisfied and the emotion or feelings being expressed. Now we have to empathise with the customer. Empathy is defined as the ability to put yourself in the other person's shoes to understand their frame of reference. It is not the same as sympathy. Sympathy means being involved in the other person's emotions, where you might lose the objective perspective.

Demonstrating the feeling of empathy for the customer is important. If we are face-to-face with the customer, empathy is somewhat easier to show. Using body language such as nodding, having a sympathetic expression, leaning towards the customer, etc can all indicate concern. It is important, however, to express empathy verbally. On the phone this is obviously even more fundamental.

The way we do this is by using specific empathy statements expressed in a tone that indicates sensitivity to the customer's feelings. It is important to tell your customer directly, and sincerely that you realise what they are going through.

Empathy technique
The technique we will use is to:

- **rephrase the content** (which means to restate the reason the customer is upset in your own words)

- **reflect the feeling** (put the emotions you are interpreting from the customer into words).

Example of format:

— It can be . . . (feeling) when . . . (content) (Content is the cause of the feeling)
— I can understand . . . (feeling) when . . . (content).

Other approaches are:

1 Are you (feeling) because . . . ?
2 You seem to be saying . . .
3 It is (feeling) when (content).
4 It sounds as if you are (feeling) because (content).
5 I would be (feeling) if this happened to me.

6   I can see you are (feeling) because (content).
7   It looks like you are (feeling) because (content).

Don't just say 'I understand'. Such a statement is a cliché. You may hear the customer say in reply 'You don't understand – you're not standing here with no bag, desperate for a change of clothes!' If you use 'I understand', make sure you include *what* you understand (the reason the customer is upset) and the *feeling* you are hearing (the emotions they are expressing).

Airline example
In the Airline example described in the active listening section, empathy statements could be as follows:

- 'I can understand your being disappointed (feeling is reflected) that your bags have been delayed' (the content restated).

- 'I would feel concerned (feeling is reflected) if I were missing all my favourite clothes (the content is restated).'

EXERCISE

Creating empathy statements
Write an empathising statement for the scenario we introduced earlier, restating the content (the reason they are upset) and reflecting the feelings (the emotions they are expressing).

Don't apologise yet! For the example, as we discussed, we want to practise each skill individually, before putting them all together. Obviously, in the real world, you would group the empathy, the apology and the resolution more closely together.

Customer situation: 'This is the third time you have promised delivery of these products and you have missed the dates.'

Write your empathy statement.

Answers
Three possible ideas are (again don't use all three!):

- I can understand you're feeling *let down* (reflect the feeling) because we *have missed the shipping dates on three occasions* (restate the content).

- It could make you *not trust* (reflect the feeling) *any dates we supply you with* (restate the content).

- It must be *difficult* (reflect the feeling) to *manage your other projects with such uncertainties about delivery* (restate the content).

Empathy bridges barriers
When you use empathy statements, you are verbally crossing to the customer's 'side' in order to demonstrate you understand their predicament. Often, when you have done this, the customer then follows you back to 'your side' to resolve the issues. 'I know this is not really your fault.' Empathy statements allow both sides to move *from their positions*: 'I work for the company,' 'I need this for my job' to instead focusing on *shared interests*: 'What do we need to do to get this problem resolved?' Empathy statements, when used effectively, are a key tool in exceeding customer expectations.

A: Apologise to the customer

Don't pass the buck
When a problem situation arises, it is tempting to avoid it or to pass the buck, to say it was someone else's fault. Even when you know the problem was created by an error on the part of someone within the company, don't assign blame to any of your company's personnel. Doing so will only reflect badly on the company as a whole, and therefore on you.

Always apologise
Often individuals are reluctant to apologise because it wasn't their fault. The point is moot – whoever's fault it was is irrelevant, you can still be sorry that the customer is disappointed with the service received. However it is important to say more than 'I'm sorry'; this is equivalent to 'I understand' in empathy statements. It is important to make the apology specific: 'I am sorry that . . .'

When travelling with a major airline recently, we were an hour late taking off from Dallas because we had to wait on the runway for a thunderstorm to clear. When we finally took off the Captain offered no apology – another dull moment of truth with an airline.

When I asked the person sitting next to me about this (also a captain en route), she said 'It is not our policy to apologise for something that is not our fault.' An interesting policy. How much more pleasant it would have been to have heard an announcement from the cabin instead 'I apologise for the delay in taking off due to the bad weather in Dallas. I will do my best to catch up some of this time on our journey.' This would not have been an admission of fault, just a politeness to smooth the journey.

Don't say 'but'

One of the largest temptations when apologising is to say 'I'm sorry, *but* the . . .' The *but* effectively negates any words that precede it in the sentence; they disqualify the apology. Many times, the reason for the mistake relates to internal problems and the customer does not want to know, or should not be told about these issues. If you want to provide an explanation, then use *however* as a bridging word, but think twice before justifying the problem.

What about when the customer is in the wrong?

Finally, remember the customer is always right even when they are wrong. They may not be right, but they are still the customer. You can still apologise for the inconvenience they are having with the situation even if the situation is of their own making.

For instance, take the example of a customer who had not followed the correct procedure to install a patch when upgrading a system. As a result the system failed. Obviously, if they had followed the correct procedure the system would have worked. It does not help to tell the customer that! They are probably already kicking themselves because of their mistake. It is perfectly acceptable to say 'I'm sorry the installation did not go well – let's look at how we can make it a success this time.'

The end result from the latter will be a calmer customer, more willing to work with you on the issue. When customers hear apologies it helps them calm down, and move more logically to a positive problem resolution mode.

Airlines example

To continue the example of the lost (sorry, delayed) baggage, a couple of appropriate apologies would have been:

- I'm sorry for the inconvenience the absence of your baggage is causing you.

- I apologise on behalf of the company for the delay in your baggage.

not:

- I'm sorry *but* the crew in San Francisco messed up.

- I'm sorry *but* most people get their baggage back at some time!

EXERCISE

Apologising to the customer
Using the situation discussed in the last two exercises, write how you would word an effective apology to the customer.

Customer situation: 'This is the third time you have promised delivery of these products and you have missed the dates.'

Write down your apology.

Answers

- I'm sorry we have not been able to make the delivery dates promised.

- I apologise for the inconvenience the slipped delivery dates have caused you.

R: Resolve the situation
After you have listened actively, empathised and apologised to the customer, the emotions of both parties should be under control. Now is a good time to move the focus of the interaction to resolving the situation.

In the heat of the moment it is easy to think only of a reactive solution: one that fixes the immediate problem. While this is a good start, it is important to consider more proactive options:

- Is there need for a change in a process or procedure?

- What could be done to stop this from happening in the future?

- What other sources of information could be provided to customers?

Airlines example
To complete the airline story, the reactive solution would be to create a step-by-step plan to get the baggage to the customer, for instance:

- Fill in an accurate claim form.

- Get the address of the customer.

- Check in the system for any notes on the bag.

- Send a note through the system to discover what plane it is on.

- Organise the pick-up of the bag when it arrives, and despatch it to the house.

Some of the proactive things to check could be:

- Was there a system mistake, which meant that the bag did not get on the same aeroplane?

- The centre for dealing with information and requests in the United States only takes incoming calls – perhaps the phone system should include the ability to make outgoing calls.

- What other services could we offer the customer, in the event that the process does break, to make the experience less stressful? A complete set of toiletries? Vouchers for clothes?

How did the actual airline do? In reality, on a scale of 1–10, they scored about a two on reactive service. There was no apology, no empathy. I had to call four times for updates, I had to push to discover financial compensation policies, and at the first contact (one of those fundamental moments of truth) the representative said — 'The system says your bag is here: have you checked the conveyor belt?' Obviously I wanted to not have my suitcase at 5:30 in the morning and create a problem for this person! Arguing with the customer is never a good idea.

What about a proactive solution? Based on the reactive score card, I would be very doubtful whether any system changes would be forthcoming.

EXERCISE

Creating reactive and proactive solutions

Create a reactive and proactive solution for the ongoing situation.

Customer situation: This is the third time you have promised delivery of these products and you have missed the dates.'

1 Outline a reactive solution.
2 Outline a proactive solution.

Answers
Reactive solutions:

- Talk to the people involved in giving dates.

- Get a new date.

- Ask questions about what could go wrong to prevent these dates being met.

- Commit to call the customer directly if the dates change.

Proactive solutions:

- Research what happened to the last three dates.

- Is there some change to a system that prevents slippage in dates like this from occurring?

- What new process could be introduced to ensure that the setting of dates is more accurate?

Answer
Suggested reply: 'I can understand your frustration that the dates have slipped on several occasions. I apologise for the inconvenience this may have caused you. Let's look now at a realistic date for delivery of your order.'

IMPLEMENTING THE CLEAR TECHNIQUE

Using the CLEAR technique, even with lots of practice, is not as straightforward as it looks. In the pressure of the moment it is often not easy to remain calm and address the issues in a controlled way.

CHECKLIST

1 Do you actively solicit customer complaints?
2 Do you use the CLEAR technique when dealing with angry internal or external customers?

CASE STUDIES

Kitchen Barn deals with customer complaints

Kitchen Barn set up a comprehensive system to record and track customer complaints:

- Gary reviewed all written complaints personally and replied within seven business days. Even when he was travelling, his executive assistant knew that this was critical data for him to receive.

- He would often personally call the customers with his apology, request more data and attempt to create a solution. The customers were so delighted they often forgot, or downplayed, their complaint.

- Customer complaints in the store about products were also tracked and fed back to the product development group. This group collated the data, sent the customer a card thanking them for their comments and telling them what action had been taken.

- In staff meetings sales associates role-played some of the difficult issues they faced around furniture and window coverings. From these role-plays a reference manual was created for the staff.

- Posters asking customers what Kitchen Barn could to to meet their needs more effectively were displayed in every store with suggestion cards. The same process was also implemented internally with awards being offered for the best ideas that became customer processes.

With constant review of complaints and Gary's active involvement, gathering the relevant data for process improvements became a way of life at Kitchen Barn, and service and sales continued to improve.

Internet Express deals with customer complaints

In the technical support area, over 90 per cent of the calls are related to problems – that's why the group exists. As we discussed in Chapter 6, the group had already made the first steps in creating a 'tool-box' that included suggested scripts for difficult interactions. In addition they created new systems for tracking customer complaints and issues:

- Every rep that had dealt with an irate customer was required to complete a single form that identified why the customer was upset and what the outcome of the discussion had been.

- These forms were fed into the continuous improvement efforts (see the next chapter).

- Managers made an effort to listen in to irate customer calls in order to identify whether the cause of the tension was a product issue or if it was the way the service provider was dealing with the customer.

- This data was then integrated into the manager's coaching role. (See Chapter 10 for more information.)

ACTION POINTS

1 How can you ensure your people use the CLEAR technique?

2 How do you record customer complaints, both verbal and written?

3 Who responds to complaints and in what time period?

4 How is the customer's reaction to this response tracked?

5 How could you improve the effectiveness of your complaint procedures?

9

Instituting Continuous Improvement Processes

As we discussed in Chapter 2, instituting continuous improvement is the fourth leg of the service delivery model. More often than not we implement a reactive solution to the customer's situation, while not looking any further into the root cause of any problems. We need to ensure that we also include proactive problem resolution, to prevent upsets to future customers. In addition, constantly initiating and implementing customer service task forces can help to drive customer service improvement.

MAKING LONG-TERM PROCESS IMPROVEMENTS

In order to ensure we are consistently improving existing processes, and solving a problem once rather than many times, it's important to use an effective problem-solving methodology and to constantly question systems and procedures.

Problem-solving

No matter how organised and structured the material service processes are, things break. We live in a rapidly changing world, and humans are more than capable of errors. Problems often occur. These can encompass major issues such as system faults, missed shipping deadlines, shortfalls in sales, communication issues such as conflicts and misunderstandings, and smaller mistakes such as wrong data entry, missed mini-milestones and mistakes. When any problem occurs there is a tendency to react and fix it, but sometimes the sympton gets fixed, not the root cause. Successful problem resolution involves identifying the source of the problem and then using proactive strategies to prevent it from recurring. Organisations which adopt these pro-active problem-solving approaches will save long-term and be more able to exceed customer expectations.

Proactive problem-solving involves a number of steps:

1 Perceive the problem.
2 Define the problem.
3 Analyse the problem.
4 Generate alternatives.
5 Evaluate alternatives.
6 Make a decision and implement.

Below are some ideas for questions to ask, and guidelines for approaching each step in this process. Examples of this process in action are included in the case studies later in the chapter.

Problem-solving step	Questions	Guidelines
Perceive the problem	• Is there a problem? • What does it look like? • Where is the problem?	• Don't assume a problem is bad • Look for the real problem
Define the problem	• What are the facets of the problem? • Is it a tangible problem (missing deadlines, sales targets)? • Is it an intangible problem (conflicts)?	• Avoid assumptions • Create a problem definition that —is specific and measurable —shows how the problem relates to the customer and the organisation
Analyse the problem	• What is the problem and what are the symptoms of the problem? • What is really the root cause?	• Don't jump to resolution too quickly • Use an analysis tool such as a fishbone diagram
Generate alternatives	• How could we approach this problem differently? • What are some new ideas?	• Generate as many ideas as possible • Record all ideas • No criticising • Everyone participates

	• What are ideas we tried once before but could adapt?	• Combine and build on ideas
Evaluate alternatives	• What criteria shall we use? • How will we weight options? • How will we balance objective and subjective criteria?	• Make sure the criteria are verbalised • Listen to all team members' input • Be aware of win-lose tactics
Make a decision and implement	• To what extent is this solution satisfactory to all? • Do we have time to care?	• Try for a win-win solution • Consider other restraints such as time and resources

EXERCISE

Solving a problem

Analyse a current problem that is affecting service to the customer and work through the process to identify some possible solutions. Think carefully about the underlying root cause of the problem.

1 Perceive the problem: what is the problem?
2 Define the problem: be specific. Make sure you find the root cause.
3 Analyse the problem: what are the components of it?
4 Generate alternatives: what are some possibilities, both conventional and unconventional?
5 Evaluate alternatives: what criteria will you be using to decide on a solution?
6 Make a decision and implement: who is going to do what by then?

ESTABLISHING CUSTOMER SERVICE TASK FORCES

Many organisations decide when they institute the customer service initiative to establish customer service task forces. These teams play several important roles in driving up customer service levels:

- They involve a broader spectrum of people often from diverse groups within the company.

- They are able to make recommendations and implement specific process improvements.

- They keep customer service 'in sight and mind'.

In order for these customer service task forces to have a chance at being successful there are certain requirements:

1 Senior management must be committed to the task forces, listen to their input, and empower them to make changes.
2 Each task force needs to have a trained facilitator – many such groups fail because there is no one person trained to guide the group process.
3 The task force must be allowed time to work on their allocated task. This sounds obvious, but it is amazing how many managers expect such work to be conducted above and beyond their employees' normal workload.
4 Time needs to be invested in ensuring that the right skill and experience mix is included on each task force. Being alive is not the only requirement!

With these qualifications met, the task forces can prove to be an active and effective tool in helping the company to delight the customer.

CHECKLIST

1 Have you analysed a current problem that is affecting service to the customer?
2 Have you any customer service task forces?

CASE STUDIES

Kitchen Barn: continuous improvement

Kitchen Barn undertook a more proactive problem-solving approach with customer complaints:

- Customer complaints in the store about products were tracked and fed back to the Product Development group. This group collated the data, sent the customer a card thanking them for their comments and telling them what action had been taken.

- GUEST implementation teams were established in every district. Their role was to monitor the customer and employee suggestions and recommend improvements to management. With the success of the GUEST teams and the application of the proactive problem-solving methodology, continuous improvement became a way of life at Kitchen Barn.

Internet Express: continuous improvement

Problem-solving
Internet Express, high-tech computer software support centre was supporting over 30,000 customers covering over 50 products. Initially Arthur advocated the problem-solving approach for his team. An example of a problem faced between two groups is shown below. Theresa was the manager of the group in question, the first-level support group that takes all incoming calls.

1 Perceive the problem
The customers began complaining that the response time (time to answer the phone) was not quick enough and that problems were taking too long to fix within the first-line support group. Arthur began tracking performance data regularly, which showed the deterioration in response time, and raised the issue with Theresa. Theresa initially believed that such issues had arisen before and that there was no need to take immediate action. As the situation continued she realised that this time the problem was longer running than in previous times and that action should be taken.

2 Define the problem
In the short-term two problems were defined:

- On average the phone is being answered at . . . time, with . . . staff and . . . resources.

- Average time from the problem being called in, to the problem being solved, has risen from three to six days . . . customers are complaining about poor service.

3 Analyse the problem
Categories to help adequately define the problem were as follows:

- time of day

- type of calls

- time to answer the call

- type of problem

- people on site

- other tasks individuals were performing, etc.

4 Generate alternatives
Options generated initially included:

- change the phone answering process

- use voicemail more frequently

- reprogramme ACD (automatic call distributor) to allocate call flow more effectively

- create a new group to answer the phone

- reorganise the group.

   In this part of the problem-solving process, the possible challenges in addressing the issues arose. Theresa was reluctant to consider the approaches that would result in major reorganisation of her team. She believed she had built a cohesive unit and did not want to change the structure just for the sake of change. In involving Arthur's management team in generating ideas, Sharon, a manager from another group, expressed that she had a completely new idea for how the team could operate and be successful. Arthur was impressed by the possible innovative way out of the problem.

5 Evaluate alternatives
The team created a list of criteria on which to make a decision.
Theresa presented a logical cause and effect analysis, with which
Arthur agreed.

6 Make a decision and implement
As a result, the decision was made to try several short-term
solutions (changing resource allocation, bringing in temporary
help for paperwork, etc), implement these and then monitor for
performance improvement.

The call volume went down within a short time (it had been
driven by a new product release and customers asking questions
on additional features) and this short-term response was a success.
This analysis prevented the team from hiring new people, always a
time-consuming and expensive process, when a more short-term
resolution was better.

Establishing project teams
However, as the organisation continued to re-evaluate its existing
processes and procedures, Arthur became aware of the need to
structure the approach to continuous improvement by establishing
specific project teams.

The challenge for Arthur's team was to move from purely
reactive technical support to a more proactive approach. The
management team tended to be more junior, and loved the excitement and the challenge of the dynamic technical support
environment. Every day was different! Unfortunately, they
mistook their reactive mode for productivity, a common mistake,
and as a result were not as focused on the long-term issues as they
could have been.

For this reason, Arthur divided his management group into
four long-term process improvement teams:

- measurements and metrics
- service level agreements
- product knowledge and training
- escalation process.

Any issues that arose in any of those areas were filtered to that
team so as to centralise the information.

ACTION POINTS

1   How can you ensure the root cause of problems is tackled, and the core problem solved?

2   Pick one problem with which to try out the problem-solving approach. What worked? What was the most difficult step? Which was the most valuable step? What was the greatest benefit in using this approach?

3   How often do you regularly evaluate your internal systems and procedures? What questions can you create to ensure the validity of material service processes?

4   When can you establish customer service task forces to keep the momentum of the service initiative alive? Who could be included? How would you monitor their effectiveness?

10

Helping Managers Become Leaders

As we discussed in Chapter 2, managers are the driving force behind the customer service culture change. If they lead the process by 'walking the talk' then they act not only as role models, but are also critical in directing process improvements and coaching team members. They need to be both managers and leaders. They need to do the day-to-day activities with their employees as well as lead from the front. In this chapter we explain and clarify the differences between a manager and a leader, and show the contributions they can make as leaders to the service initiative.

WHAT IS LEADERSHIP?

The critical characteristics for leaders fall into three categories:

- achieving the objective
- developing the individuals
- building the team.

Leaders help the team to achieve the objective by focusing on results and by doing 'real work' themselves. Leaders build the team by leading only when necessary and engaging the team throughout the stages of team development. Leaders also develop the individuals on the team by getting the whole team energised with their charisma and inclusive attitude of 'we' not 'I'. A careful examination of each of these areas (see Figure 6) will build an understanding of how leaders drive the customer service improvement process.

ACHIEVING THE OBJECTIVE: FOCUS ON RESULTS

The leader plays an important role in helping to achieve customer service goals in two main arenas. First, the leader defines specific

Fig. 6.   Role of the customer service leader.

objectives, sets customer service standards, and measures and monitors results. In this way the leader charts and checks the course to reaching the results expected (much of this was discussed in Chapter 7). Secondly, the leader is responsible for many 'behind the scenes' actions needed to remove the barriers to delivering exceptional service.

One of the more subtle aspects of this role is serving as the link between the organisation and the team. This link spans several areas that include helping to reduce or eliminate barriers to customer service, ensuring the team has the resources it needs to perform effectively, and acting as the main communication channel between the team and the rest of the organisation and its customers.

Managers can undertake a wide range of activities to ensure their people can exceed customer expectations. These activities can include:

- obtaining access to resources (update hardware, software, improve phone system, etc)

- making sure service providers have the information they need
- negotiating with other organisational teams
- intervening when material service delivery processes are inhibiting personal service
- sifting through 'organisational politics'.

Creating the right environment is a crucial part of the 'real work' the leader must do, so that results can be produced.

EXERCISE

Using a chart like the one below, think about the current challenges your team faces in delivering exceptional service. Factors could be lack of resources, problems with systems, etc. List them in the left-hand column.

Factors inhibiting service delivery	Possible actions for you

Now brainstorm actions you could take to reduce or eliminate some of these factors and write them down in the right-hand column. Be prepared to share the list with your team members for feedback and ideas.

UNLEASHING INDIVIDUALS' ABILITIES

As we discussed in Chapter 4, building the correct skill mix is significant for providing exceptional service. However, once the service providers are hired the constant monitoring of talent and developing of individuals becomes paramount. Coach team members constantly. By getting team members excited about what they are there to do and coaching their performance with proper feedback, the leader unleashes the hidden abilities of his/her people.

INDIVIDUAL COACHING PRINCIPLES

When meeting with team members to provide feedback it is important to prepare the coaching session in advance, to ensure a balance is achieved between positive and developmental feedback. The following are some guidelines to optimise a coaching session.

1   Think about the person you are meeting with.
2   Think about the area you wish to address. Be specific about the details in terms of either the positive behaviour and/or the behaviour you wish to improve. Ensure you have adequate support data.
3   Think about balancing the good news and the bad news to ensure the team member's self-esteem is protected.

Use the following checklist to guide you through the coaching process.

❏	**Coaching steps**
❏	+ Start with a positive
❏	1 Agree on agenda
❏ ❏	2 Get team member's input: • Skills being handled well • Skills needing improvement
❏ ❏	3 Give your feedback: • Skills being handled well • Skills needing improvement
❏	4 Develop action plan together
❏	5 Confirm actions and checkpoints

You will see in the case studies the tools the managers developed to coach their teams more effectively in the service delivery process.

BUILDING THE TEAM

According to Katzenbach and Smith in their bestseller *The Wisdom of Teams*:

> 'A team is a **small number of people** with **complementary skills** who are committed to a **common purpose, performance goals**, and **approach**, for which they hold themselves **mutually accountable**.'

Teams that have maximised their SCORE when providing service have been found to contain the following characteristics:

S: Cohesive **S**trategy and direction (see Chapter 3)

- A customer service strategy aligned with the company vision and mission.

- Clearly articulated values and ground rules for providing service.

- An understanding of risks and opportunities facing the team in delivering service.

- A clear categorisation of key result areas, particularly in relation to customer service.

C: **C**lear roles and responsibilities

- Clear definition of team members' roles and responsibilities.

- The team's responsibility is shared by all members.

- Specific and measurable objectives to measure individual results (see Chapter 7).

O: **O**pen and honest communication

- Respect for individual differences.

- An open and non-judgemental communication environment among team members.

R: **R**apid response to change

- A rapid response to the customers' needs as well as internal problems (see chapter 9).

- An ability to manage and respond to change in the internal and external environment.

E: **E**ffective leadership

- A team leader who is able to help service providers achieve the task, develop individuals and build the team.

EXERCISE

What is your team SCORE in delivering exceptional service?

Step 1 Review the questions in each section and indicate to what extent, for each category, you are meeting the prerequisites for a customer-focused team.
1 = very clear/successful 10 = not clear at all/not successful

Step 2 Ask the rest of the team, individually, to also rate each characteristic in the same manner.

Step 3 Create an average for the specific elements. Discuss each one in turn and identify why individuals have rated them in that way and what could be done to improve each rating.

Step 4 Discuss any marked differences in rankings. For instance, if one person rated open, honest communication as a nine and another as a two, discuss the reasons for the disparity.

How easy will it be for your team to raise the SCORE in delighting your customers?

Rating: 1 = very clear/successful
            10 = not clear/not successful

Characteristic	Rating
Cohesive **S**trategy and direction • To what extent is your customer service strategy in alignment with the corporate vision and mission? • To what extent can everyone in your team repeat your customer service mantra? • To what extent is your team adhering to its values? *Overall rating in this category*	

Characteristic	Rating
Clear roles and responsibilities • To what extent have you ensured that your team has the correct skill sets? • To what extent are team members clear about their individual key result areas? • To what extent are team members' workloads accurately reflected in their objectives? *Overall rating in this category*	
Open and honest communication • To what extent do your team members communicate effectively with each other? • To what extent do your team members communicate about feelings? • To what extent do your team members try to adapt their styles when communicating with each other? *Overall rating in this category*	
Rapid response to change • To what extent does your team recognise, define and analyse potential customer problems? • To what extent does your team generate creative problem-solving options? • To what extent does the team adapt to external changes? *Overall rating in this category*	
Effective leadership • How successful are you at 'running interference' so that your team can complete its work and meet customer needs? • To what extent are you providing relevant feedback to team members? • To what extent are you continually motivating team members? *Overall rating in this category*	

RECOGNISING ACHIEVEMENTS

The manager can help to sustain long-term focus and motivation by instituting and implementing effective reward and recognition systems. This can help raise excitement and commitment to a service culture.

There is a temptation, when the customer service initiative is performing well, 'to leave well enough alone'. Unfortunately delighting your customers requires consistent recognition of individual and group accomplishments.

Too often organisations and individuals view achievements as completion of major milestones. Achievements can also consist of multitudes of moments of truth; small successes that occur every single day. These achievements and moments of truth can occur in both the material (getting the work done) and personal (interacting effectively with the customer) service aspects. Although we experience many of these positive moments of truth per day, instead of recognising them and celebrating them we tend to focus on what has not worked, thereby reducing individual confidence and lowering motivation levels.

> By recognising and celebrating accomplishments, service organisations not only build cohesiveness but also positively raise trust and morale.

In the future, keep your eyes open for those positive moments of truth that you can use to build team spirit and therefore ultimately improve customer service. Awareness of these achievements is the first step in being able to celebrate successes.

CELEBRATING SUCCESS

Celebrating achievements provides a sense of well-being and builds morale within the company. Celebrating achievements can be as simple as having a meal together, or as sophisticated as organising an off-site event for team members at an innovative location. Ideas for celebrations are listed below. The list is by no means complete!!

- team dinner
- picnic
- barbecue
- social events after work
- give-aways such as sweatshirts, T-shirts, water bottles, etc
- awards
- certificates
- service provider of the month
- complementary time off
- celebrate key milestones with cake, cookies, etc
- outdoors experiential event
- other team training
- off-sites.

EXERCISE

Celebrating achievements

Step 1 Identify two achievements in exceeding customer expectations. They can be smaller moments of truth or larger project accomplishments.

Step 2 Decide at least *two ways* you will celebrate *each* achievement you just identified.

CHECKLIST

1 Did you look at the factors that are inhibiting service delivery on which you could take action?
2 Did you evaluate your team SCORE?
3 Did you decide ways to celebrate achievements?

CASE STUDIES

Kitchen Barn: turning managers into leaders

Achieve the objectives: intervening to support customer service
The management team of district managers and regional managers had played an integral role in setting service objectives and standards for their stores, as described in Chapter 7.

Their role became pivotal in intervening in the technical data arena so that their teams could provide customer service. The traditional market of kitchen and housewares had a thorough training manual and plenty of written documentation to which sales associates could refer. However, selling furniture required different technical data and more in-depth knowledge of such things as window coverings, wood, beds, etc. None of this information was available in a clear, easily understandable format.

The district managers created a proposal, allotted funds and instituted an in-depth, modular technical training programme that was rolled out to all store personnel over a six-month period. Some of the material was taught in group sessions, often by vendors. Much was in self-teach modules, with tests that the students reviewed with their managers.

The implementation of this programme was an outstanding example of how managers can intervene, from behind the scenes, to help in the external service delivery process.

Develop the individuals: coaching and motivation
The group constantly offered awards for exceptional service, such as free products, single-item focus competitions (SIFs) and, at the annual conference, a Sales Associate of the year award would be presented.

Build the team: the SCORE assessment
Each district team, and then the team within each store, completed the SCORE assessment within a four-week time frame. This assessment was then used in varying ways:

- Each district compared the SCORE ratings for each store. Not only did this provide an indication of the teams that were motivated, but there was a strong correlation between the team assessment and the perceived competencies of the store managers by the district manager. Not surprisingly, the store managers who were perceived as strong by the district manager normally had strong teams, and vice versa. This tended to validate the district manager's opinion.

- Occasionally, the district manager's assessment of the store manager was different from the team's SCORE. For instance, one of the store managers was not well respected, but the team rated itself very highly. This gave the district manager an opportunity to discuss with the team members the reasons for their ratings. In her research she discovered that the store manager was really doing a good job: there had been just one conflict with one of the merchandising managers, which had coloured the store manager's credibility.

- Different districts within the same region also compared their results, with the same outcome. It provided the regional manager with an additional source of data about the performance of her district managers.

- As a result, many of the stores initiated a greater focus on strategy, and planned specific store events to build trust and communication within the teams.

Internet Express: turning managers into leaders

Turning the management team into leaders
Many of the managers in Internet Express were young with no direct management experience. As a result most of the managers were very technically-oriented, with a limited understanding of the complexity of managing large teams. Arthur recognised this challenge and undertook several approaches to help his team become leaders:

- He asked the training company that had presented the Managing Customer Perceptions programme to develop and roll out a coaching programme to his managers.

- He consciously went outside the company to recruit some individuals from other organisations to add more balance to his management team.

- He contracted with a consultant in the short-term, to provide some 'instant-depth' in managing a support function. This consultant was able to work with the existing management team and suggest a range of improvements, resulting in new ideas, as well as the management team learning at the same time.

- He made some tough decisions in terms of changing the job roles of two individuals who were struggling with the complexity of managing large teams. One he managed to reassign as a project manager, the other decided to move to another start-up where he could make more of an impact.

Achieve the objectives: intervening to support customer service
One of the biggest barriers to exceeding customer expectations for the technical support group was the release by the engineering group of products that appeared to be 'riddled with bugs'. The management team realised that the technicians could only do so much on the phone if the quality was seriously lacking.

Each member of the management team picked one of the product areas, and made it their priority to build closer working relationships with the development group responsible for that product. In this way they not only ensured a greater access to development engineers to resolve difficult problems, but they also were able to get a 'heads-up' on future issues. The support team then could institute some sort of proactive fix, such as a patch, a work-around, etc and avoid some of the customer frustrations.

Develop the individuals: coaching and motivation
The leadership team established a standard call-monitoring worksheet to ensure that the skills taught in the programme were reinforced on a regular basis. The standard was established that all technical support engineers should have one call a month monitored anonymously (the engineer was not aware that the manager was listening in). Although this did not sound like a heavy commitment, managers found that they would have to listen to several calls before they were able to listen to a call when the rep was able to practise the full range of skills on the assessment.

Initially the engineers were resistant to the call monitoring because they believed it implied a criticism of their current performance. When they started to receive positive feedback and rewards (night on the town for the best call in a month), they reduced their negativity and began to compete on who could do best!

Build the team: the SCORE assessment

When the team completed the SCORE assessment they discovered that the customer service strategy was still unclear to many of the team members, despite the efforts that had been made to communicate it. They therefore initiated a new communications campaign that included posters, cards, T-shirts and sweatshirts to spread the word again.

The SCORE assessment also indicated that the leadership team was divided by conflicts between two functional groups and their managers. Arthur invested in taking the team off-site where he combined a strategy session with a team profiling seminar. The team was profiled using temperament and the Myers Briggs Type Indicator (described in the book *Turning Team Performance Inside-Out*). This data provided an objective framework from which to understand the individual differences among team members, and communication and teamwork improved as a result.

ACTION POINTS

1 How will you ensure that your managers lead rather than direct?

2 What else can you do to help the managers develop as customer service coaches (develop the individual)? Do they need specific training in coaching skills?

3 What could you do to raise team cohesiveness, in order to improve service effectiveness?

4 What else could you do to celebrate successes? What type of reward and recognition systems could you implement to help to sustain the customer service focus?

Summary

As we have seen, delivering exceptional service requires a clear customer service strategy, effective internal standards and processes, customer-focused people using competent inter-personal skills, continuous improvement and managers who lead the initiative. The main message is – delighting the customer is an ongoing process. It never ends.

DELIGHTING THE CUSTOMER

As we've discussed throughout the entire book, 'going the extra mile' can leave a memorable impression that the customer talks about time and time again. It is these types of stories that create a reputation in the marketplace for exceptional service and help to build long-term viability for a business.

Legendary service is not restricted to large chains. Small companies can also delight the customer. Think of those situations where small restaurants where you eat regularly greet you by name, local copy shops offer advice at no charge to tidy up a newsletter, your coffee shop makes your coffee for you with-out asking what you want. As a customer, receiving exceptional service is a rewarding experience. Let's finish with my favourite story of being delighted as a customer.

Nick's restaurant in Maui at the Kea Lani Hotel prides itself on delighting its clientele. One of the examples is when it 'spikes its customers'.

Imagine yourself sitting in a restaurant. You are trying to decide what wine would go best with dinner. You are talking to your partner debating the various merits of different bottles. The manager comes to the table to take your order (this alone is unusual on a Saturday evening.) You tell your wine selection to him – lo and behold, he brings the bottle of wine that you have selected from behind his back. You have just been spiked!

Such a moment of truth required a series of interconnected actions:

- A leader committed to exceeding customer requirements.

- A clear strategy on delivering exceptional service.

- A process to listen to individual customers as they discussed their wine choice.

- People who were committed and rewarded by exceeding customer expectations.

- Constant review of processes to ensure no stone was left unturned in delighting the customer.

We have quoted this story to many people as an example of a small organisation that made a commitment to customer service and delighted the customer. Wouldn't you like your customers to say the same thing about your business?

If your answer is yes – the answer is in your hands. Follow the steps in the book and you will keep your customers coming back to you. Good luck in the process!

Further Reading

If It Ain't Broke, BREAK IT, Robert J. Kriegel and Louis Patler, Warner Books, 1999

Direct From Dell, Michael Dell, Harperbusiness, 1999

The Brain Book, Peter Russell, Routledge, 1979

Service America: Doing Business In the New Economy, Warner Books, 1995

Moments of Truth, Jan Carlzon, HarperCollins, 1989

Getting Past No, William Ury, Bantam Doubleday Dell Publications, 1993

Getting Results! The Secret of Motivating Yourself and Others, Michael LeBoeuf, Berkeley Publications Group, 1994

What America Does Right: Learning From Companies That Put People First, Robert H. Waterman, New York, Norton, 1994

The Age of Unreason, Charles Handy, Harvard Business School Press, 1991.

Getting To Yes: Negotiating Agreement Without Giving In, Roger Fisher, William Ury, Bruce Patton, Penguin, 1991

The Seven Habits of Highly Effective People, Stephen R. Covey, Simon & Schuster, 1989

The Wisdom of Teams, J. Katzenbach & D.K. Smith, New York, HarperCollins, 1993

Language Within Language: Immediacy, a Channel in Verbal Communication, Morton Wiener, Albert Mehrabian, Irvington Publications, 1968

The 5 Pillar of TQM: How To Make Total Quality Management Work For You, Bill Creech, Plume, 1995

Turning Team Performance Inside-Out, Susan Nash, Davis Black Publishing, 1999

Games Teams Play, L. Berdaly, McGraw Hill, New York, 1996

How to Win Customers and Keep Them for Life, Michael Leboeuf 1989.

Index